HIP-HOP

A CULTURAL AND MUSICAL REVOLUTION

THE MUSIC LIBRARY

By Vanessa Oswald

Portions of this book originally appeared in
The History of Rap and Hip-Hop by Soren Baker.

Published in 2019 by
Lucent Press, an Imprint of Greenhaven Publishing, LLC
353 3rd Avenue
Suite 255
New York, NY 10010

Copyright © 2019 Greenhaven Press, a part of Gale, Cengage Learning
Gale and Greenhaven Press are registered trademarks used herein under license.

All new materials copyright © 2019 Lucent Press, an Imprint of Greenhaven Publishing, LLC.

All rights reserved. No part of this book may be reproduced in any form without permission in writing from the publisher, except by a reviewer.

Designer: Deanna Paternostro
Editor: Vanessa Oswald

Library of Congress Cataloging-in-Publication Data

Names: Oswald, Vanessa, author.
Title: Hip-hop : a cultural and musical revolution / Vanessa Oswald.
Description: New York : Lucent Press, [2019] | Series: The music library |
  Includes bibliographical references and index.
Identifiers: LCCN 2018020132 (print) | LCCN 2018022417 (ebook) | ISBN
  9781534565166 (eBook) | ISBN 9781534565159 (library bound book) | ISBN
  9781534565142 (pbk. book)
Subjects: LCSH: Rap (Music)–History and criticism. | Hip-hop.
Classification: LCC ML3531 (ebook) | LCC ML3531 .O8 2019 (print) | DDC
  782.421649–dc23
LC record available at https://lccn.loc.gov/2018020132

Printed in the United States of America

CPSIA compliance information: Batch #BW19KL: For further information contact Greenhaven Publishing LLC, New York, New York at 1-844-317-7404.

Please visit our website, www.greenhavenpublishing.com. For a free color catalog of all our high-quality books, call toll free 1-844-317-7404 or fax 1-844-317-7405.

Table of Contents

Foreword	4
Introduction Hip-Hop Philosophy	6
Chapter One The Emergence of Hip-Hop Culture	10
Chapter Two Hip-Hop Goes National	20
Chapter Three Rap Music	31
Chapter Four Introduction of Gangsta Rap	42
Chapter Five The Rap Business Expands	54
Chapter Six Southern Rap and the Reemergence of DJs	65
Chapter Seven The New Global Rap Landscape	76
Notes	90
Essential Albums	95
For More Information	97
Index	99
Picture Credits	103
About the Author	104

Foreword

Music has a unique ability to speak to people on a deeply personal level and to bring people together. Whether it is experienced through playing a favorite song on a smartphone or at a live concert surrounded by thousands of screaming fans, music creates a powerful connection that sends songs to the top of the charts and artists to the heights of fame.

Music history traces the evolution of those songs and artists. Each generation of musicians builds on the one that came before, and a strong understanding of the artists of the past can help inspire the musical superstars of the future to continue to push boundaries and break new ground.

A closer look at the history of a musical genre also reveals its impact on culture and world events. Music has inspired social change and ignited cultural revolutions. It does more than simply reflect the world; it helps to shape the world.

Music is often considered a universal language. A great song or album speaks to people regardless of age, race, economic status, or nationality. Music from various artists, genres, countries, and time periods might seem completely different at first, but certain themes can be found in all kinds of music: love and loss, success and failure, and life and death. In discovering these similarities, music fans are able to see how many things we all have in common.

Each style of music has its own story, and those stories are filled with colorful characters, shocking events, and songs with true staying power. The Music Library presents those stories to readers with the help of those who know the stories best—music critics, historians, and artists. Annotated quotes by these experts give readers an inside look at a wide variety of musical styles—from early hip-hop and classic country to today's chart-topping pop hits and indie rock favorites. Readers with a passion for music—whether they are headbangers or lovers of

Latin music—will discover fun facts about their favorite artists and gain a deeper appreciation for how those artists were influenced by the ones who paved the way in the past.

The Music Library is also designed to serve as an accessible introduction to unfamiliar genres. Suggestions for additional books and websites to explore for more information inspire readers to dive even further into the topics, and the essential albums in each genre are compiled for superfans and new listeners to enjoy. Photographs of some of music's biggest names of the past and present fill the pages, placing readers in the middle of music history.

All music tells a story. Those stories connect people from different places, cultures, and time periods. In understanding the history of the stories told through music, readers discover an exciting way of looking at the past and develop a deeper appreciation for different voices.

INTRODUCTION

Hip-Hop
Philosophy

The roots of hip-hop culture stretch back more than 40 years; however, this movement is still recognized as a fairly new addition to modern culture. This particular culture is one that is self-made and constantly evolving. Some people claim that hip-hop is dead; however, it still lives, just in different ways than how it may have started out.

Hip-hop grew from its humble beginnings in the South Bronx section of New York City into a significant and influential cultural movement. Created in the mid-1970s by poor Bronx residents with few resources, hip-hop has become a billion-dollar industry with a worldwide reach. Hip-hop has influenced the way people make music, the way they dance, and the way they wear their clothes. It has also shaped people's political views and turned many people into entrepreneurs.

Four Elements of Hip-Hop

Hip-hop culture encompasses four main components: rapping (MCing), disc jockeying (DJing), graffiti art, and break dancing (B-boying). At its beginning, hip-hop was inspired by a variety of other art forms, many of which still influence and inspire hip-hop artists today. One of hip-hop's key characteristics is its ability to take an idea, a practice, or a way of doing something and make it into something new.

For instance, spoken-word poets who recited rhyming lyrics over a musical backing, such as the Last Poets, Gil Scott-Heron, and Rudy Ray Moore, were among the group of performers who are often considered the first generation of rappers. Each of them infused their poetry with political commentary. Their work included condemnation of white oppression, insults to then-President Ronald Reagan, and support of the black power movement.

Early hip-hop DJs invented a new way to enjoy music by repeating song passages best suited for dancing, while graffiti artists went from writing their names on buildings and billboards to creating dazzling art showcased in galleries. B-boys, also known as boogie boys or break-dancers, created a new style of dance featuring acrobatic skills.

Rap Takes Over

The most popular component of hip-hop culture is rap. Even though the words "hip-hop" and "rap" are often used interchangeably, they are not the same thing. Rap is part of a larger culture, while hip-hop is the culture itself. When people refer to hip-hop music, they typically mean rap, even though hip-hop music also includes other musical genres, such as rhythm and blues (R&B), soul, funk, jazz, and even rock and roll.

The first major rap recording was "Rapper's Delight," which was released in 1979 by the Sugarhill Gang. Just five years later, rap music was the dominant part of hip-hop culture. In early rap recordings, rappers typically performed over music made by musicians who simply copied the original music of other artists. By the mid-1980s, however, sampling and advances in technology and studio equipment (most significantly drum machines) changed the way rap was made. Sampling allowed producers, the people in rap who make the music, to incorporate segments of the original recordings of other artists into the producers' own material. Today, rap is made in a number of ways, including sampling and playing live music.

The Sugarhill Gang released the first major rap recording "Rapper's Delight" in 1979.

The way in which people rap has also evolved. Rappers in the 1970s favored a simple, straightforward style. The lyrics of most early rap songs focused on having a good time and boasted about the ability of a DJ or the lyrical skills of the rapper. By the mid-1980s, known as the golden era of rap, rappers had developed complex deliveries and a number of rhyme styles to complement the explosion in sounds and kinds of music being produced. In the 1990s, rap became largely regional, with New York rappers focusing on lyricism; Los Angeles, California, rappers focusing on gangster (or "gangsta") themes; and southern artists boasting of their heritage. Today, rappers make songs about virtually everything.

Hip-Hop Lifestyle

Hip-hop's influence on popular culture has been immense. It is an integral part of the lives of millions of people worldwide. Classes on hip-hop culture and on the work of such rappers as 2Pac (also known as Tupac Shakur) are taught in a number of major American universities. Rap artists join their rock-and-roll contemporaries on tour and in performances at major sporting events such as the Super Bowl and the NBA All-Star Game. Hip-hop songs are among the most popular ringtones for cell phones, and hip-hop artists contribute to the soundtracks for video games and movies.

However, hip-hop has also endured its share of doubters and controversy. In its formative years, hip-hop culture, along with its various manifestations, was dismissed as a fad. Embraced by the young generation, it created a rift with parents who thought rap was not music, graffiti was not art, and break dancing was not dancing. Furthermore, as rap became popular, at times, many activists claimed it had a negative influence. Feminist groups have criticized the misogynistic lyrics of some rappers; religious figures have criticized the violent, "thuggish" work of gangsta rap artists; and civil rights organizations have boycotted several rappers because of their homophobic lyrics.

Despite these detractors, hip-hop has provided a sense of hope and purpose for millions of people. Hip-hop is considered by its practitioners and followers as the voice of the voiceless, the voice of youth, and a major cultural force. Hip-hop has given a generation of people hope that they could become successful and respected in any number of ways, whether by winning a DJ tournament, designing acclaimed artwork, choreographing the dance moves for a music video, starting their own

JAY-Z is one of the most successful modern-day rappers in hip-hop.

business, or becoming a famous rapper.

Indeed, JAY-Z, Dr. Dre, and Diddy are part of the select group of artists who are no longer looked at as just rappers. They are now superstar personalities, entertainers who are among the most respected and powerful celebrities in the world. They all had a desire to make it as rappers, to be successful in their lives, and to achieve the American dream—and they all did it with the musical and cultural force known as hip-hop.

CHAPTER ONE

The Emergence of Hip-Hop Culture

The general public has repeatedly misunderstood hip-hop culture and segments of its history, several areas of which have been up for debate, such as creators of certain methods. The movement began in the mid-1970s in the Bronx, an impoverished section of New York City inhabited by a large segment of lower-class black Americans and Latinx people. The increasingly poor borough was disintegrating because of crime, arson, housing abandonment, and overall neglect by its residents and their landlords. Many vacant, crumbling, high-rise apartment buildings provided an ideal haven for illegal activities, including drug dealing, robbery, and murder.

Amid this chaos, a group of young black and Latinx Bronx residents with few economic resources and a need to express themselves created their own entertainment with the materials available to them. They played the record collections of their parents to entertain themselves, they used the cardboard boxes littering the streets as dancing surfaces, and they used cans of spray paint to make their own art. The result was the birth of a new culture: hip-hop.

Hip-hop culture includes rapping, DJing, graffiti art, and B-boying, also known as break dancing. Rappers recite words over music; DJs are people who play and comment on recorded music, either on the radio, in dance clubs, or at concerts; and break-dancers perform an energetic style of dance that often includes exaggerated body movements and acrobatic moves, such as headspins. One of the earliest ways that hip-hop culture found expression, however, was through graffiti.

Graffiti Trend

Though illegal, graffiti became popular in Philadelphia, Pennsylvania, in the 1960s as a way for people to express themselves in public places. By the 1970s, it had spread to New York City. Some graffiti artists, also known as writers or "graffers," were members of street gangs who wrote their gang names on walls and benches to mark their territory. Other graffiti artists who were not in gangs promoted themselves as artists by creating their own nicknames, or tags, to accompany their drawings. A few artists paid homage to their neighborhood by including in their tag the number of the street on which they lived. For example, some of the early graffiti artists were TAKI 183, Joe 136, Julio 204, and Frank 207.

These graffiti artists often used bright colors to enhance their designs. They wrote their tags in a number of different styles, from basic print or cursive writing to more elaborate forms that included calligraphy-like designs and shading. Regardless of the design, the point of graffiti was for it to be seen, so the artists made sure that the color of the paint they used was visible against the wall or backdrop on which they painted.

Graffiti writers made their biggest mark on the subway trains that traveled throughout the New York metropolitan area. While trains were parked in the train yard at night, graffiti writers went to work painting their exteriors. To the artists, subway cars were large, mobile canvases.

Although the people doing it saw graffiti as art, others did not share this view. People living in the wealthier sections of New York City looked at graffiti as a symbol of the decay of their city. People living in graffiti-filled areas expressed displeasure over the art, which defaced buildings and reduced the attractiveness and value of property in their neighborhoods. They also were upset with the gang members who used graffiti to mark their territory. However, in the desolate Bronx environment, many young people turned to graffiti as a source of entertainment. They used it not only as a means of self-expression, but also, since it was illegal, as a way to rebel against the government that they felt ignored their desperate plight.

DJ Kool Herc Creates a Culture

Most of the graffiti artists had similar musical tastes. By listening to music, they and other young residents of the Bronx could temporarily escape their abysmal surroundings. These residents listened to soul artists such as Al Green and Marvin Gaye, funk practitioners James Brown and George Clinton, disco acts such as the Bee Gees and Chic, and the electronic group Kraftwerk, among many others.

One of these young music fans was Clive Campbell, better known by his stage name, DJ Kool Herc. He was born in Kingston, on the Caribbean island of Jamaica, and grew up listening to ska and

THE EMERGENCE OF HIP-HOP CULTURE

reggae music, two energetic musical forms that originated in his homeland. An avid music fan and record collector, Herc (short for Hercules, the Greek warrior hero) was impressed by the sound systems used by DJs in Jamaica. The DJs that Herc watched as a child transported monstrous speakers and record collections to outdoor concerts given in front of hundreds, and sometimes thousands, of people.

In 1967, when he was 12, Herc immigrated with his family to the Bronx, bringing his love for music with him. As he grew up, Herc decided he wanted to become a DJ. After collecting enough records and stereo equipment, he began hosting open-invitation block parties where he played music to entertain the people. To play the music loud enough, he created a sound system that he modeled after the mobile setups he had heard and seen in Jamaica.

With the help of his friends, Herc carted his enormous speakers, which often stood up to 6 feet (1.8 m) tall, along with prized selections from his mammoth collection of more than 1,000 records to the courtyards of public housing buildings and plugged his equipment into the lampposts. This stolen electricity powered his turntables and allowed him to play music for the

DJ Kool Herc is known as one of the first hip-hop DJs who helped popularize the genre.

neighborhood for hours. Within months, the parties that Herc hosted drew an increasingly large and diverse group.

Many of the people gravitated to the parties, which were held on a smaller scale in the recreational rooms of apartment buildings, because the events were like going to a nightclub, but the attendees did not have to dress up or pay a lot for admission. The parties were also easy to get to. Some participants could simply walk outside to the courtyard of their apartment building. For others, the parties were only a subway ride away. The events were an easy and convenient gathering point for a group of people with little disposable income and few inexpensive entertainment opportunities, especially for those who enjoyed dancing.

Discovering the Breaks

Herc noticed that people who enjoyed dancing at his DJ sessions became especially animated during certain kinds of songs, particularly funk songs when the music would "break" down, having the percussion instruments playing alone. People enjoyed dancing to the breaks more than any other portion of the song. Dancers used the breaks to showcase specialized dance routines with complicated spinning and leg maneuvers.

With his DJ sessions becoming increasingly popular, Herc made a breakthrough in how a DJ works. He extended the breaks, making them the focal point of his DJ sets. To do this, he put a copy of the same song on each of his two turntables. A device known as a mixer, which DJs normally put between the two turntables to manipulate a record on one turntable without having to reach over the other turntable while it was playing, allowed Herc to switch between the two records. He would find the break on one record, play it, and then switch over to the same break section on the record on the second turntable, using a knob called a fader. Once he had practiced finding the breaks in songs, Herc could repeat them over and over again by using the mixer and fader to shift back and forth between the two copies of the same record.

The dancers at Herc's sessions loved his breaks. During these extended portions of the rhythm sections of songs, they were able to practice and experiment with moves that before had been limited to brief flashes during the climax, or high point, of a song. Intricate footwork, spinning moves, and mechanical motion were the signature moves of the dancers. For example, they did headspins by standing on their heads and spinning around with their arms outstretched and legs raised toward the sky. Another was the moonwalk, in which dancers slide backward

THE EMERGENCE OF HIP-HOP CULTURE

as their feet and legs appear to be moving forward. Pop icon Michael Jackson popularized the moonwalk during a performance of his song "Billie Jean" on the TV special *Motown 25: Yesterday, Today, Forever* on March 25, 1983.

Herc called these dancers breaking boys, since they danced to the breaks. The dancers became known as B-boys for short. The early B-boy crews included the Zulu Kings, Zulu Queens, Shaka Kings, and Shaka Queens. They traveled the Bronx and other parts of New York, going from party to party to showcase their dancing.

Godfather of Hip-Hop

The parties that Herc hosted included other DJs besides himself. Among them were Grandmaster Caz (later of the Cold Crush Brothers), Grandmaster Flash, and a young Afrika Bambaataa, who eventually earned the title of Master of Records because of his immense knowledge of a wide range of musical styles, including rock, soul, funk, R&B, and reggae. Besides being a DJ, Bambaataa was also a member of a Bronx street gang called the Black Spades. Eventually, however, Bambaataa came to believe that gang warfare was destroying his beloved city. Gangs sold drugs and killed people, and Bambaataa believed they had to be stopped. Bambaataa later reflected on the impact gangs were having in New York during the 1970s: "I saw it was time to move the gangs in a different direction, before we all wound up dead or in jail."[1] To do so, Bambaataa formed the Zulu Nation, a peaceful organization that

Afrika Bambaataa is known as the Godfather of Hip-Hop.

HIP-HOP: A CULTURAL AND MUSICAL REVOLUTION

aimed to popularize and promote the developing hip-hop culture. It adopted the motto "Peace, unity, love, happiness and fun."[2]

Using a pair of turntables his mother had bought him for his high school graduation, Bambaataa quickly established himself as one of the premier DJs of the developing hip-hop culture, with a reputation to rival that of DJ Kool Herc. He used a wide range of records from any musical style he could collect, from the fiery, funky music of James Brown to the computerized sounds of Kraftwerk. Bambaataa later became known as the Godfather of Hip-Hop.

Hip-Hop Parties Create Battles

With Herc and Bambaataa becoming celebrities in their neighborhoods, competition between DJs began to develop. DJs began unofficial rivalries with each other to see whose sound system was the loudest and whose sets were best received by the crowd. Bambaataa later recalled his early DJ sets:

> We were always trying to outdo each other, play records more obscure than any other deejay, scratching out the titles so other deejays couldn't copy us. People would tell me they didn't like salsa music, but I'd slam some on 'em with a break beat, and they'd be dancing to it. I'd work in calypso and rock, the Monkees, Kraftwerk, James Brown, and just for kicks an old Coke commercial or "My Boyfriend's Back." You came to my shows, you were going on a musical journey.[3]

The high-energy music played by renowned DJs such as DJ Kool Herc and Afrika Bambaataa transformed sets into more than just an opportunity to listen to a wide variety of sounds. At these parties, people could watch B-boy crews such as the Rock Steady Crew—the most respected B-boy group because they were known to have the best dancers. Besides watching the B-boys perform seemingly gravity-defying dance moves, attendees could observe the graffiti artists who were literally making their mark on subway trains and buildings throughout the city. The people attending these gatherings did their own unofficial recruiting by urging their friends, neighbors, and family members to join them at the hip-hop parties. However, the scene remained largely unknown to the rest of the world.

Importance of the DJ

DJs remained the stars of hip-hop gatherings, so up-and-coming DJs were eager to find ways to separate themselves from other DJs. In

Grand Wizzard Theodore was the inventor of scratching.

scratching sound. In a 2001 interview, Grand Wizzard Theodore recalled how he invented scratching:

I came home and played my music too loud and my mom was banging on the door and when she opened the door I turned the music down but the music was still playing in my headphones and she was screaming "If you don't turn the music down you better turn it off" and I had turned down the speakers but I was still holding the record and moving it back and forth listening in my headphones and I thought "This really sounded [like] something [special] … interjecting another record with another record." And as time went by I experimented with it trying other records and soon it became scratching.[4]

1975, Grand Wizzard Theodore, a high school student and aspiring DJ, developed another asset to help DJs impress audiences. Unlike DJ Kool Herc, who purposely incorporated long breaks into his DJ routine, Theodore created his addition to hip-hop culture by accident and in isolation. His invention was scratching. Scratching occurs when the DJ moves a record back and forth against the needle, creating a

Grand Wizzard Theodore also created the needle drop, an important but often overlooked DJ tactic. The needle drop occurs when a DJ drops the needle on a record at exactly the point they want the record to play without having to cue it up or listen to it. Theodore did this by looking at the record itself. Records are partially made out of vinyl. On each side is one long, continuous groove that circles the record dozens of times. When certain musical changes, such as a guitar solo, take place in a song, the spacing between the coils of the groove changes, becoming either wider or narrower. After listening to a song several times, a DJ can look at the vinyl, tell by the spacing where such musical changes occur, and thus know where to drop the needle to play a desired section.

As more DJs entered the hip-hop field, they continued to develop, refine, and enhance their routines. The use of breaks, scratching, and needle drops, among other techniques, enlivened the DJs' sets. The DJ had evolved from someone who simply played records and worked a crowd to someone who knew how to keep partygoers dancing from the start of the party until the last song was played. As the one in control of the party, the DJ was the center of hip-hop culture, which got its name because of the way the dancers would "hip" and "hop" (jump and move) to the music.

MCs Surface

To keep the crowds entertained during breaks in their sets, the DJs hooked up microphones to their sound systems and spoke to the audience. They said simple phrases such as "And ya don't stop" and "To the beat, y'all." However, during the sets themselves, the DJs, who had to focus on

BOOM BOX POPULARITY

Around 1980, personal stereos became a popular way for people in New York to listen to music while they were outside. These personal stereos, known as boom boxes because the music would "boom" from the speakers, could easily be carried from one location to the next. They typically got both AM and FM radio stations and had either one or two cassette decks. Cassette tapes from early hip-hop events were often played on these personal stereos.

During this time, only a few rap songs had been released and there were no radio shows dedicated to playing rap music. This made the boom box essential for rap music to be heard throughout New York City. Indeed, the mobility of the boom box allowed rap to spread quickly throughout the streets of New York, as a person could carry it along on the subway, into a store while shopping, or onto a basketball court while watching a game. Boom box owners personalized their stereos by adding a strap so they could sling it over their shoulder or by tagging the boom box with graffiti.

THE EMERGENCE OF HIP-HOP CULTURE 17

keeping the party going by playing the right records, had their friends keep the crowd engaged by talking into the microphone. Such a vocalist was called an MC, short for master of ceremonies; this is where the rapper originated from.

At first, the main purpose of the MC was to praise the DJ. For instance, an MC might say that Grandmaster Flash "cuts faster" than the competition, meaning that he could cut, or scratch, more effectively and efficiently than other DJs. "Grandmaster cuts faster" also sounded clever because it rhymed. The MC in this instance was thus rhyming and praising Grandmaster Flash simultaneously.

The MCs soon became popular attractions and started talking more frequently during the parties. They often spoke in rhyme and engaged in call-and-response with their audience. For example, the MC would say to the crowd, "Everybody say, hey!" and those in attendance would respond by yelling "Hey!" This call-and-response created a lively atmosphere, similar to that found in some churches, and made the audience feel as though they were part of the entertainment, not just being entertained. The MCs also popularized famous sayings such as "Throw your hands in the air like you just don't care."

By the late 1970s, the MCs were becoming stars in their own right and were drawing their own crowds. DJs and club and party promoters began pitting aspiring MCs against each other in sharp exchanges of wit called battles. Now, instead of making the DJ the focus of the action by rapping about partying and the merits of their skills, the MCs competed for the spotlight against each other. Like the DJs before them, MCs took great pride in being able to entertain crowds and deliver the most memorable rhymes, which often included boasts about their rhyming abilities.

During the MC battles, the art of freestyle rhyming evolved. This kind of rapping is defined by MCs who make up rhymes on the spot. Typically, these clever performers describe the room they are rhyming in, the crowd they are performing for, or the clothing or look of their opponent, which they often criticize.

Out from the Underground

MCs could use the bragging rights from a battle to land hosting gigs at area clubs and even headline their own shows. Club managers started hiring DJs and MCs, now also called rappers because of the way they would rap (slang for "converse" or "talk") with their audience, because it was clear that they could draw crowds. Some of the early clubs that showcased rap were Harlem World, Disco Fever, and the Rock Steady Lounge. The success of these shows convinced the entrepreneurs among the DJs, rappers, and club owners that they could sell recordings of the events. Soon, cassette tapes featuring the work of the emerging DJs and rappers in New York City spread across the country as people shared them with friends and relatives.

People no longer had to attend a party or a hip-hop night at a club in New York City to engage in the hip-hop experience. This new style of music that consisted of breaks and rappers speaking in rhymes over the music to an energetic audience excited fans. Hip-hop then went from an underground phenomenon into a movement, which caught the eyes of music executives eager to make a profit from it.

CHAPTER TWO

Hip-Hop
Goes National

In the beginning, hip-hop culture was primarily an underground New York scene, which included DJs such as Grandmaster Flash and DJ Hollywood, and rappers such as Busy Bee and Mele Mel (sometimes spelled Melle Mel) who drew hundreds of people to nightclubs. Block parties hosted by DJ Kool Herc, Afrika Bambaataa, and others remained popular gathering places for B-boys, graffiti artists, and aspiring DJs and rappers. However, there was no formal introduction to this musical phenomenon until the late 1970s. Propelled by a host of creative and energetic artists, this early stage of hip-hop culture was one event away from emerging on a national scale. That event was the release of a song called "Rapper's Delight."

Sugarhill Gang

Rap and hip-hop took a major step forward in 1979 with the release of "Rapper's Delight" by the Sugarhill Gang. It was only the second rap song ever recorded and released commercially. (The first was "King Tim III [Personality Jock]" by the Fatback Band, and it had only been released a few weeks before "Rapper's Delight.") Sugar Hill Records owner Sylvia Robinson, who had been a successful R&B singer and songwriter before becoming a record company executive, wanted to record a novelty record she hoped would cash in on the hip-hop trend. She assembled three little-known rappers—Wonder Mike, Master Gee, and Big Bank Hank—and had them record a song. The result, "Rapper's Delight," which borrows its groove from "Good Times" by the disco group Chic, became a smash hit.

Each rapper contributed simple, playful lyrics that welcomed everyone to the hip-hop world. Early in his first verse, Wonder Mike invites people of all races and nationalities to join the group's musical party. The Sugarhill Gang fills the rest of the song with other themes that many people could relate to: a love of flashy fashion, the desire to attract members of the opposite sex, and the awkwardness of having an uncomfortable experience with a friend.

Several future music superstars were among the more than 2 million people who bought a copy of the single. In fact, "Rapper's Delight" was the first record that popular R&B singer Mary J. Blige, who rose to fame in the 1990s, ever bought. She explained, "It was the newest thing, so everyone was running to get it."5

sold, and enjoyed on a national scale. Less than a year later, Kurtis Blow became the first rapper to get a recording contract with a major record company, when he signed with Mercury Records in 1979. It was a major accomplishment for the genre, which at that time was still a virtually unknown commodity. Another breakthrough came in 1981, when the Funky 4+1, a rap group best known for their single "That's the Joint," was featured on the hit

Rap Breaks into the Mainstream

"Rapper's Delight" eventually reached number 36 on the pop singles chart and peaked at number 4 on the R&B chart. The popular song was many people's introduction to rap. After all, anyone who did not live in or visit the New York metropolitan area could not experience hip-hop culture firsthand.

The success of "Rapper's Delight" convinced a few record company executives that this new form of music could be profitable. The song demonstrated that this new art form could be mass-produced, bought,

The Funky 4+1 was the first hip-hop group to perform on Saturday Night Live.

HIP-HOP GOES NATIONAL   21

comedy sketch program *Saturday Night Live*, thereby becoming the first rap group to make a national television appearance.

Most major corporations and media entities, however, ignored rap. They looked at the new form of music as a fad, like disco, that would soon disappear. This lack of interest from corporate America forced rap, much like rock and roll before it, to develop without the influence of major record companies.

"The Message" of Hip-Hop

Sugar Hill Records used the success of "Rapper's Delight" to become a prominent rap label. The Sugarhill Gang followed up the song with the 1980 single "8th Wonder," which peaked at number 15 on the R&B charts, and the 1981 single "Apache," which peaked at number 13 on the R&B charts. However, the next landmark release from Sugar Hill Records came from Grandmaster Flash and the Furious Five, a respected rap collective anchored by renowned DJ Grandmaster Flash and rapper Mele Mel. The group released "The Message" on the label in 1982. It became one of the most influential and significant rap singles of all time.

Unlike the few commercially released rap songs that preceded it, "The Message" describes the desolate neighborhoods that many members of hip-hop culture called home. It is a dark, serious song that stands in stark contrast to the party music, brimming with arrogance, that most rappers were releasing at the time.

Grandmaster Flash and the Furious Five released "The Message" in 1982.

THE GET DOWN

In August 2016, the Netflix show *The Get Down* premiered. The period musical drama, created by Baz Luhrmann and Stephen Adly Guirgis, is set in the 1970s and follows a group of teenagers in the South Bronx during the rise of hip-hop culture. Content for the show is a mixture of fictional and real stories, all inspired by the emergence of this new culture, which brought hip-hop and rap to the forefront of music and society. *The Get Down* was canceled after just one season.

Joseph Saddler, otherwise known as Grandmaster Flash—a prominent DJ at the start of hip-hop culture—served first as a consultant for the show, then a producer, and he was also a character on the show played by actor Mamoudou Athie. Flash commented on his contributions to hip-hop and its effect on the rest of the world:

> This thing we did in the South Bronx has affected millions of people around the world. So it has been an ultimate pleasure to be a part of this and to touch so many people, people who don't even speak the language. Like, The Get Down was released in 190 different countries, in 30 different languages. So now, this era becomes a topic of discussion. It's wonderful to give people a chance to see it and to talk about it.[1]

1. Quoted in Shawn Setaro, "Grandmaster Flash Talks 'The Get Down,' Hip-Hop History and More," *Forbes*, October 20, 2016. www.forbes.com/sites/shawnsetaro/2016/10/20/grandmaster-flash-the-get-down-more/#6859cea55b31.

A number of prominent rappers, from gangsta rap pioneer Schoolly D to respected lyricist Common, cite "The Message" as their reason to rhyme. Gangsta rapper Jayo Felony recalled the impact that "The Message" and Mele Mel made on his life:

"The Message," that's when I finally really got into writing raps, when I heard that song … that was like the first time I heard somebody say anything like that and the raps he was talking about were real street. "Don't push me, 'cause I'm close to the edge/I'm trying not to lose my head." That song inspired me to rap.[6]

Rap Style Gets More Complex

In addition to the darker tone of "The Message," people were drawn to the song because the rhymes of Mele Mel were more sophisticated and complicated than those of other rappers such as the Sugarhill Gang or Kurtis Blow. Mel was a seasoned veteran of the mid-1970s rap circuit who won a number of rhyming battles because of his ability to construct complex rhymes.

HIP-HOP GOES NATIONAL

Grandmaster Mele Mel's rhymes were more complicated than many other rappers.

members favored a simple pattern that often incorporated obvious rhymes, such as "cat" with "hat" or "feet" and "seat." Other rappers, such as Busy Bee and Kurtis Blow, favored a similarly simple, good-natured, laid-back rhyming approach that could not keep up with the lyrical advance of rappers such as Mele Mel, Kool Moe Dee of the Treacherous Three, or T La Rock, whose multisyllabic words and fast delivery patterns required great skill to perform without stumbling over the lyrics.

A Different Sound

Even though "Rapper's Delight" is a party hit and "The Message" reflects the harsh reality of living in an American ghetto, the two songs share a number of similarities. Like most of the rap music from this period, the use of instruments in these songs was minimal. Unlike songs in other genres of music, which included a variety of instruments (sometimes with intricate progressions), rap music of this era typically featured only drums, a bass line, and maybe

With a commanding voice, interesting rhymes, and an intimidating stage presence, Mel (also known as Grandmaster Mele Mel) was the type of rapper that other rappers aspired to be. He was articulate, clever, tough, and, most of all, respected by the hip-hop community.

By contrast, the Sugarhill Gang

a keyboard effect or two. Unless the songs were recorded with a house band, as was the case with some of the recordings produced by Sugar Hill Records, few other instruments were used.

Part of the reason rap artists used minimal instrumentation was that, as outsiders in the music business, they lacked access to state-of-the-art studios. Instead, they often recorded music in amateur home studios that did not have the capability to produce complex, layered recording favored by established studios. Therefore, rappers not backed by a house band often did their rhyming over only a drum track that came from a drum machine, which is a piece of studio equipment that makes a variety of drum sounds.

Many musicians and record company executives said that rap, with its sparse sound and style, was not music because its songs do not contain melody, which is a rhythmically organized sequence of single tones so related to one another as to make up a particular musical passage or idea. In fact, many R&B and funk artists went out of their way in interviews to discredit rap music.

However, the criticism did not stop rap from evolving. Afrika Bambaataa's 1981 single with the Jazzy Five, "Jazzy Sensation," set the stage for his landmark work with Soul Sonic Force. Their 1982 single "Planet Rock," which borrows the melody from Kraftwerk's "Trans-Europe Express," helped pioneer a new sound that relied on keyboards and electronic sound effects to accent the music. Many of these sounds recalled a computer blip or the chirping of birds. Bambaataa and his group rapped and sang much in the way that old funk bands did: intermittently, with computer-altered voices and with long breaks in which the music played uninterrupted. Bambaataa later recalled how he invented his new sound, which he called "electro-funk":

I learned from James [Brown], Sly [Stone] and Uncle George [Clinton] ... But I was also listening to Yellow Magic Orchestra, Kraftwerk and Gary Numan, and ... the electronic music in John Carpenter's "Halloween" movies and "Assault on Precinct 13." I wanted to be the first black group to come out with that sound. So I formed [Soul Sonic] Force and invented electro-funk.[7]

Hip-Hop on the Silver Screen

As rap evolved with new sounds and styles, graffiti, B-boying, and DJing were also making major contributions to hip-hop culture. The festive video for "Rapper's Delight" features B-boys showcasing some of their dance moves, while the gritty video for "The Message" takes place on a rundown city street with buildings covered with graffiti.

The 1983 film *Wild Style* shows how connected each component of hip-hop was at that point. The movie has several story lines, among them the struggle that a graffiti writer goes through to balance his personal life with his love for his art. The movie features graffiti-writers, rappers, DJs, and B-boys in prominent roles, giving attention to each segment of the flourishing hip-hop culture. *Wild Style*, the first authentic and earnest look at the culture, is considered the definitive hip-hop movie.

Much as cassette tapes and "Rapper's Delight" had done a few years earlier, *Wild Style* gave many people their first exposure to hip-hop. However, *Wild Style* was especially significant because it provided a visual look at the culture. Now, people could imitate the graffiti artists, rappers, and B-boys they saw on screen, allowing hip-hop to grow quickly in the underground and also leading to the 1983 graffiti film *Style Wars*.

B-boying Stands Out

While rap was looked at with skepticism by the mainstream

The Rock Steady Crew was one of the first break-dancing crews formed. Many of their members were featured in movies.

HIP-HOP: A CULTURAL AND MUSICAL REVOLUTION

business world, B-boying was the first element of hip-hop culture to be embraced by corporate America. Released in 1983, the hit film *Flashdance*, starring Jennifer Beals as an aspiring ballet dancer, also features Crazy Legs, Mr. Freeze, and Prince Ken Swift, members of the B-boy group Rock Steady Crew.

The next year, *Breakin'* hit movie theaters. The film centers on a jazz dancer and two B-boys who team up and become popular street dancers. Television commercials, endorsements, and other deals soon followed for B-boys who had gained media attention from their film and in-person performances. Hip-hop documentary film producer and one-time professional B-boy QD3 recalled the impact of B-boys: "B-boying was the first thing that drew attention to hip-hop, period. It was really the spark that made it go mainstream. Before that it was contained. *Flashdance* came out and break dancing was the bridge that we crossed to go into the rest of the world to some degree. [Break-dancers] were the first superstars."[8]

Rap Reaches Radio and TV

As B-boying and graffiti were enjoying commercial exposure, rap was making strides of its own. By October 1983, both Mr. Magic and Kool DJ Red Alert, prominent DJs in the hip-hop community, had radio shows on the New York airwaves. These shows, the first commercial radio outlets to showcase rap music, were critical in spreading the genre throughout New York and the rest of the country. A person who had never heard a rap song could now turn on the radio and hear entire programs dedicated to rap. In fact, many of Mr. Magic's and Kool DJ Red Alert's radio shows were recorded and shared among rap fans, much like the recordings of early rap performances.

Also in 1983 came the debut of *Video Music Box*. Entrepreneur Ralph McDaniels of Brooklyn, a section of New York City, hosted the music video show, which aired on public television and at the time was the only program showing hip-hop videos. The first video the program aired was "Five Minutes of Funk" by rap trio Whodini.

The breakthrough of rap on radio and video provided the perfect platform for Kurtis Blow. On his 1984 hit "Basketball," the good-natured rapper cleverly weaves the names of basketball stars such as Dr. J and Moses Malone into his rap about his love for the sport. The video for the song, which features Blow rapping on a basketball court, was one of the early examples of a rap song that gathered considerable attention from those not in the hip-hop audience.

With all elements of hip-hop

culture making their mark in society, rappers started touring, particularly in Europe, where the culture was openly embraced. In 1982, Afrika Bambaataa organized the first European hip-hop tour. He later recalled his world vision for hip-hop: "I was taking music from all over the planet to spread this new sound all over the planet … I wanted to break it in the Tri-State area, then across the U.S.A. and then the world. I had a vision that this was more than just party music for the ghetto."[9]

Birth of DJs and Rappers

As DJs, rap songs, and rap artists began to enjoy more success in the mid-1980s, graffiti and B-boying became little more than gimmicks to corporate America. Graffiti was still illegal, and even though some graffiti artists were commissioned, they had to paint in a controlled, often indoor environment that removed the rebellious edge of the art.

As the art world started looking elsewhere for cutting-edge work, B-boys also started losing some of their popularity. Instructional break dancing tapes were sold on television, making it seem as though anyone who bought the tapes and a dancing mat could be an instant B-boy star. In reality, it took years of practice for B-boys to perfect their moves; however, companies eager to cash in on the break dancing trend portrayed these extraordinary dance skills as easy to master.

Although break dancing became common in mainstream culture, rap was still an art form on the fringes. Major labels had yet to fully embrace the new music, allowing independent record companies such as Sugar Hill, Jive, Reality, Profile, and Tommy Boy to corner the rap market. These small companies, free to pursue any artists they deemed worthy without having to worry about approval from a corporation, signed a variety of rap talent that reflected the diverse range of people who made up the hip-hop community.

The rap trio Whodini, for example, wrote creative, narrative raps about social outcasts and love that were performed over keyboard-driven music, while Doug E. Fresh showcased his beatboxing skills on a number of his early recordings. Beatboxing is the art of using the mouth to create percussion sounds that serve as a beat for someone else to rap to. This style of making music enjoyed exposure in several 1980s movies, including the comedies *Police Academy* and *Disorderlies*, which starred the rap group Fat Boys.

However, the breakout group of this era was Run-DMC. This trio from Queens, a borough of New York City, featured rappers Run (Joseph Simmons) and DMC

Run-DMC was one of the first hip-hop groups to break into the mainstream.

(Darryl McDaniels), and DJ Jam Master Jay (Jason Mizell). The first release from the group was the influential 1983 double-single "It's Like That" and "Sucker MC's." The group presented themselves as common guys on the street who had much in common with their fans. Run, who later became an ordained minister and changed his name to Reverend Run, recalled, "One big part of [Run-DMC's] success was our catchy rhymes that made you think or sometimes laugh. No violence or harsh language, just thinking, laughing, and having fun."[10]

Hip-Hop Embraced by Other Artists

As Run-DMC helped expand rap's commercial base in the early 1980s, musicians who appreciated the grassroots nature of rap also embraced the emerging music, giving it some credibility in the musical community. Debbie Harry rapped on "Rapture," a 1981 single from her rock group, Blondie, in which she mentions hip-hop celebrity Fab 5 Freddy and uses the hip-hop slang word "fly," which is another way to say that someone or something is cool. Jazz musician Herbie Hancock teamed with Grand Mixer

HIP-HOP GOES NATIONAL   29

D.ST (who later changed his name to GrandMixer DXT) for the 1983 hit "Rockit." The video for that song features D.ST scratching and was the first time most people saw a DJ performing a scratch. R&B singer Chaka Khan featured Mele Mel on her 1984 single "I Feel for You," marking the first time that an established R&B singer collaborated with a rapper on a single.

Each of these singles gave different audiences an opportunity to experience hip-hop culture when paired with a type of music they already enjoyed. Music fans no longer had to seek out rap. It was popping up in a variety of other music styles. With rock, jazz, and R&B musicians embracing it, rap and hip-hop culture was slowly increasing in visibility and influence. Rap music was even being showcased in mainstream publications, such as rock magazine *Spin* and the *Village Voice*, which is a respected New York–based weekly newspaper. This exposure of the genre gave outsiders a better idea of what hip-hop culture had to offer and encouraged the movement's artists to push themselves creatively. As more independent record companies began releasing rap songs, hip-hop's popularity kept increasing.

CHAPTER THREE

Rap Music

The call-and-response and rhyming acts of the 1970s built the foundation upon which hip-hop culture stood. By 1984, rappers such as Run-DMC, Kurtis Blow, Whodini, and Fat Boys had made a name for themselves as hip-hop lyricists. They also continued to popularize the genre enough to acquire performance spots on the first-ever national rap tour, called the *Fresh Fest*. Other than Run-DMC, however, this set of acts was about to be replaced during the golden era of rap, which lasted from approximately 1986 to 1989.

During this period, rap enjoyed an explosion in the range, skill, and talent of rappers. Rappers focused on a variety of lyrical topics and presented themselves in a variety of forms, representing virtually every segment of society. Rappers of this era went well beyond the elementary party rhymes that the first and second generations of rappers had often employed, crafting ingenious raps about everything from dating to government corruption.

Rap Becomes Main Focus

As rap enjoyed a creative explosion during the golden era, the other three components of hip-hop culture began to fade from the spotlight, especially B-boying and graffiti. Although both survived, they were marginalized by rappers and, to a lesser extent, DJs.

The DJ was still a prominent part of live performances by providing input on the music. However, for the first time, the other elements of hip-hop were used merely to supplement the rapper. For example, there might be a set of B-boys dancing in a rap video, but they were no longer the focal point. Rappers and the music they were producing were now taking center stage.

Sampling Method

In the early years of rap, artists such

as the Sugarhill Gang, Grandmaster Flash and the Furious Five, and Kurtis Blow often rapped over live instrumentation that borrowed guitar rhythms, bass lines, and drum patterns from other songs, including, most famously, the Sugarhill Gang's usage of Chic's "Good Times" for "Rapper's Delight."

Following this habit of duplicating other artists' music, rap producers in the golden era of rap began "sampling" other songs, a practice that would permanently alter the direction of rap. Sampling occurs when a portion of a song from another recording is copied onto a piece of studio equipment called a sampler, which allows the original piece of music to be used on a new record. It is literally a sample of the original song. By using this technique, the rappers and their producers no longer needed to have musicians actually play music in order to make a song.

Samples typically last from 4 to 8 measures, but they can also be shorter or longer, depending on the wishes of the artist or producer. The samples are often matched with a drum pattern, also potentially sampled, that fits the same tempo. In addition to samples of music, samples of singers, speeches, sound effects, and other noises and sounds are used. For instance, the screeching of soul singer James Brown was a favorite sample of early rap producers.

Raising Hell

Run-DMC was one of the major beneficiaries of the idea of sampling. The group's third album, 1986's *Raising Hell*, became a multiplatinum (meaning 2 million albums were sold) success thanks in large part to the song "Walk This Way," a collaboration with the rock group Aerosmith. Run-DMC originally planned on sampling the guitar riff Aerosmith had used on its song of the same name a decade earlier. However, after producer Rick Rubin contacted Aerosmith, it was decided that Run-DMC would perform with guitarist Joe Perry and singer Steven Tyler on "Walk This Way."

With "Walk This Way," rap and rock created common ground that gathered the interest of fans of each genre. The video for "Walk This Way" marked a breakthrough in rap's development, as it was played in heavy rotation on the music video channel MTV. For many people not already interested in rap, "Walk This Way" was the first rap song that they enjoyed, and the video gave them their first taste of hip-hop fashion. Run-DMC had been developing their look, which featured all-black hats, jeans, jackets, gold chains, and white Adidas sneakers without shoelaces, for years.

Another *Raising Hell* single was "My Adidas." Here, Run-DMC pays homage to, or respects and acknowledges, its favorite shoe and, in effect, identifies itself with the brand. Musician and producer Sean "Diddy" Combs, a Run-DMC fan, recalled seeing the group perform when he was a kid: "I was at the *Raising Hell* Tour at Madison Square Garden [in 1986], and Run-DMC held up their Adidas and told everybody in the crowd to hold up their Adidas," he said. "I swear, 20,000 people held up their sneakers. I remember I was like, 'I wanna do that one day.'"[11]

LL Cool J

The music of Run-DMC was mostly gritty, aggressive, and bombastic, typical of rap music at the time. Even though the group had a sizable female following, some women found rap too abrasive, loud, and unrefined. Many women felt as though no rapper was speaking to them.

LL Cool J, whose stage name stands for "Ladies Love Cool James," filled that void by catering to women in some of his music and soon became rap's first heartthrob. His debut album, 1985's *Radio*, was better known for rugged selections such as "I Can't Live Without My Radio," "Rock the Bells," and "I Need a Beat" than his songs geared toward women, such as "Dear Yvette" and "I Want You." With the release of "I Need Love" two years later, however, LL Cool J was established as a ladies' man.

LL Cool J endured criticism from the rap community for making hip-hop love songs. Many of his

LL Cool J was rap's first heartthrob and arrived on the hip-hop scene at a time when women felt that rappers were not speaking to them.

detractors felt that, by making love songs, LL Cool J was taking away rap's edge. Nonetheless, his albums also contained several harder-edged hip-hop songs that appealed to rap fans of either gender eager to hear his clever rhymes and aggressive beats. By taking a creative risk, LL Cool J expanded rap's lyrical scope and almost single-handedly brought rap a new wave of female fans.

The rapper also transitioned into the acting world in the late 1990s. He starred in films such as *In Too Deep*, *Any Given Sunday*, *S.W.A.T.*, *Mindhunters*, and *Edison*. As of 2018, he plays the role of NCIS Special Agent Sam Hanna on the CBS crime drama TV series *NCIS: Los Angeles* and serves as the host for the musical reality competition TV series *Lip Sync Battle*.

Female Rappers

During the golden era of rap, when LL Cool J was rising to stardom, the previously male-dominated rap genre experienced an explosion of female talent. These female rappers increased rap's fan base and expanded their reach by making music that was not as abrasive and confrontational as their male counterparts.

Salt-N-Pepa became the first female rap stars. Rappers Salt and Pepa, along with rapper and DJ Spinderella, who joined the group after the release of their breakthrough debut album, 1986's *Hot Cool & Vicious*, had a string of hit singles that gave female rappers credibility. The dance song "Push It" became a party favorite. For the first time, a female rap group was respected. Writer Stephen Thomas Erlewine explained on the AllMusic website:

As the first all-female rap crew (even their DJs were women) of importance, the group broke down a number of doors for women in hip-hop. They were also one of the first rap artists to cross over into the pop mainstream, laying the groundwork for the music's widespread acceptance in the early '90s ... their songs were primarily party and love anthems, driven by big beats and interlaced with vaguely pro-feminist lyrics that seemed more powerful when delivered by the charismatic ... trio.[12]

Their song "Let's Talk About Sex" promoted safe sex, while "Whatta Man" was about praising men who treat their partners with respect. The topics brought up in rapper Queen Latifah's music also touched on issues faced by women, such as domestic violence, street harassment, and relationship problems.

MC Lyte, another credible female rapper, broke through in 1988 with the impassioned "I Cram to Understand U" single, which is part

Salt-N-Pepa was one of the first successful female rap groups.

feelings and I just respect that in anybody in the craft that can do it. OK, you're the best at what you do and that's great, but then also have other things going on that you don't mind discussing."[13] The Brooklyn-based artist is the first solo female rapper to earn a gold single, for 1993's "Ruffneck." In a genre quick to dispose of its pioneers, she has maintained her status as one of the most respected female rappers of all time.

Other notable early female rappers include MC Sha Rock, Antoinette, the late Ms. Melodie, Monie Love, Jean Grae, and The Lady Of Rage. However, one female MC who paved the way and was undoubtedly an inspiration for all rappers was Roxanne Shanté.

love song, part antidrug story. In her later material, MC Lyte raps about everything from the damaging impact of drugs to being in love, showing female rappers' versatility. "From the very beginning, I knew that there are many different sides to me," Lyte said. "In recording the very first record, it was OK to be vulnerable on record. It was OK to talk about your

Rap Recognized as Poetry

As Run-DMC, LL Cool J, and female rappers earned more attention, other rappers of the golden era were becoming more proficient, creating detailed rhymes that used complicated schemes and imagery.

RAP MUSIC 35

ROXANNE SHANTÉ AND THE "DISS" TRACK

Since the 1970s, rappers battled against one another in live settings. In 1981, Kool Moe Dee defeated Busy Bee in one of the most famous live rap battles. As rap began to be recorded, the battles took on a new form: the response record. Many artists launched their careers by responding to the songs of other rappers, even though most of the time these responses were not justified—or even provoked.

Lolita Shanté Gooden, known by her rap name Roxanne Shanté, grew up in the Queensbridge Projects of Queens, New York, and started rapping at the age of 10. Her rap career was launched at 14 years

Roxanne Shanté was one of rap's first female MCs. She began rapping at the age of 10.

The artists, their followers, and even a few journalists started considering rappers poets, a step that signaled that rappers were now being taken seriously by the media.

Three of the most respected rappers of this era, and the ones who arguably possessed the best poetic and storytelling abilities, were Rakim, Slick Rick, and Big Daddy Kane. Unlike most other rappers, who favored energetic deliveries, Rakim rapped in a laid-back but commanding tone. Rakim and his partner, DJ Eric B., released *Paid in Full*, their debut album, in 1987. The poetic power of Rakim is evident on the song "I Know You Got Soul," in which he raps about becoming one with the paper on which he writes his rhymes.

Whereas Rakim was typically serious, London-born rapper Slick Rick first gained attention in 1985 old after releasing her own response record, sometimes called a "diss" or battle track, called "Roxanne's Revenge," with producer and DJ Marley Marl. She recorded the track after UTFO's 1984 hit "Roxanne, Roxanne," in which each of the three rappers in the group explained their different reasons for wanting the fictional Roxanne as their girlfriend. Even though Shanté had nothing to do with and had no reason to take offense to the song by UTFO, her response helped pave the way for the long list of response records that followed.

After achieving this moment in the spotlight, Shanté was propelled into what became known as the "Roxanne Wars," which were a series of rap battles associated with the character of "Roxanne." UTFO decided to release an answer record featuring a female rapper who was named the Real Roxanne, first featuring Elease Jack, who was later replaced by Adelaida Martinez. Over the next year, between 30 and 100 answer records were released by different artists involving "Roxanne" in their raps.

In March 2018, the Netflix movie *Roxanne Roxanne* was released. The biopic tells the story of Roxanne Shanté, played by actress Chanté Adams, and how she became one of the first female rappers to find success in the rap scene in a heavily male-dominated industry. It also uncovers the abuse she had to overcome as a young female rapper and how her management failed to compensate her when she first started rapping. By age 25, Shanté had retired from the music industry.

as MC Ricky D through his work with Doug E. Fresh & the Get Fresh Crew on their songs "The Show" and "La Di Da Di," both of which feature Rick's creative storytelling ability and his humorous outlook on life. In 1988, Slick Rick released his dynamic debut album, *The Great Adventures of Slick Rick*. Resembling a series of short stories set to music, the album features Slick Rick taking listeners on journeys that are cautionary ("Children's Story"), inspirational ("Hey Young World"), and wistful ("Teenage Love").

Rakim had poise and Slick Rick had humor, but Big Daddy Kane was possibly the most well-rounded rapper during this time. The Brooklyn-bred rapper established himself as a tough-talking artist whose lyrical skills dazzled hardcore hip-hop followers and whose good looks made him attractive to

Big Daddy Kane is known as one of the most iconic MCs from rap's golden era.

women. His first two albums, 1988's masterful *Long Live the Kane* and 1989's *It's a Big Daddy Thing*, showcase one of Kane's biggest strengths: his diversity. He was equally skilled when rhyming about his lyrical ability ("Raw," "Ain't No Half-Steppin'"), instilling pride and hope in the hopeless ("Word to the Mother [Land]," "Another Victory"), and imagining a better world ("I'll Take You There").

As rap journalist and editor Reginald C. Dennis wrote in the liner notes of *The Very Best of Big Daddy Kane* in 2001,

> Describing Big Daddy Kane's place in hip-hop history is like pondering the accomplishments of Miles Davis or Muhammad Ali. Both were incredibly powerful presences, even without Miles playing a note or Ali stepping into the ring ... And in the end what they did wasn't as important as how they did it. They were just vessels for the truth—and the truth, as we all know, is magnetic. And so was Big Daddy Kane.[14]

An artist conscious that his music had an impact on his followers, Kane made a point of including political and social messages in his music, giving his poetry a purpose. "I wasn't one of those artists where people throw my song on and just dance to it," he said. "People actually listened to the lyrics. Because of that, I thought that [having messages in my music] was something that I should get across."[15]

Rap's Political Landscape

Rappers during the late 1980s were mindful that their words could have an impact on their listeners. Bronx rap group Boogie Down Productions (BDP) released the confrontational *Criminal Minded* in 1987 and, after the murder of group member DJ Scott La Rock, the politically-minded album *By All Means Necessary* the following year. The album features powerful songs about the need for peace, the impact of political corruption, and the importance of safe sex.

BDP helped create a brand of rap later labeled "conscious rap," which incorporated political and social commentary and often spoke of revolting against the government and other agencies that the artists considered oppressive. The movement also included Brand Nubian, X Clan, and Poor Righteous Teachers. The most popular and arguably the most influential group of the conscious rap movement, however, was Public Enemy. After releasing the sizzling *Yo! Bum Rush the Show* in 1987, the group released, a year later, what

Public Enemy is known as one of the most influential rap groups of all time.

RAP MUSIC 39

many music critics consider the best rap album of all time, *It Takes a Nation of Millions to Hold Us Back*. As Erlewine wrote in AllMusic,

> Public Enemy rewrote the rules of hip-hop, becoming the most influential and controversial rap group of the late '80s and, for many, the definitive rap group of all time ... [They] pioneered a variation of hardcore rap that was musically and politically revolutionary. With his powerful, authoritative baritone, lead rapper Chuck D rhymed about all kinds of social problems, particularly those plaguing the black community, often condoning revolutionary tactics and social activism. In the process, he directed hip-hop toward an explicitly self-aware, pro-black consciousness that became the culture's signature throughout the next decade.[16]

Rap Transcends

Whereas Public Enemy, BDP, and others had a militaristic bent to their politically infused music, the rap collective Native Tongues (whose members included Jungle Brothers, De La Soul, A Tribe Called Quest, and Queen Latifah, among others) put more playful and inspiring but less confrontational messages in their music. The members of the collective promoted peace, justice, and equality, but their music made it clear that they were going to enjoy themselves, too.

Although each member of Native Tongues was important, De La Soul had the greatest impact on rap's development, especially with their first album, 1989's *3 Feet High and Rising*. De La Soul changed the composition of rap albums by incorporating humorous skits, which were included throughout their debut album. These skits were not songs, but rather interludes that featured group members participating in a humorous game show. Today, many rap albums typically have at least one skit.

In addition to Native Tongues, other New York rap groups were making tremendous creative strides. Gang Starr, for instance, was one of the first rap groups to incorporate jazz music into their work, while Stetsasonic called themselves the "hip-hop band" because they used live instruments during their recordings and performances, something unheard of in the era of sampling. The comical and controversial Beastie Boys demonstrated for the first time that white rappers could create quality rap music and be respected by members of the rap community. Nonetheless, some critics and rap fans treated the Beastie Boys as a novelty act because their members were white and used juvenile humor in their music.

Rap Develops Outside New York

White rappers were not the only ones looking to join the rap world. In the late 1980s, after the success of Run-DMC, LL Cool J, Salt-N-Pepa, Beastie Boys, and several movies depicting hip-hop culture, rappers from cities besides New York began making their own brand of rap music. Artists from these other cities experimented with sound, rap style, and lyrical content, continuing rap's creative development and adding new elements to the genre.

In Philadelphia, Pennsylvania, DJ Jazzy Jeff & the Fresh Prince, the good-natured rap duo whose playful songs "Parents Just Don't Understand" and "A Nightmare on My Street" were quality examples of profanity-free rap, demonstrated that the genre did not have to be confrontational. The duo also created the theme song titled "Yo Home to Bel-Air" for the 1990s TV sitcom *The Fresh Prince of Bel-Air*, starring the Fresh Prince, otherwise known as Will Smith.

In Los Angeles, California, King Tee (also spelled King T) delivered a California interpretation of New York's boastful style of rap, while MC Shy D helped put Atlanta, Georgia, on the map with his up-tempo party raps.

These rap artists who hailed from outside of New York were helping to develop a rap scene nationally that would help spread the hip-hop movement. Even though rappers in New York had started the hip-hop movement, others outside of that city were being influenced by the culture and were looking to add their own styles to make the genre even more diverse. This addition of new artists led to a new rap revolution.

CHAPTER FOUR

Introduction of Gangsta Rap

Once the golden era of rap took its final bow in the late 1980s, it was replaced with a new kind of rap, which was more explosive and controversial and led to many different responses from critics inside and outside the music community. This more explicit and profane brand of rap would become known as gangsta rap. In the early days of gangsta rap, rappers who performed it presented themselves as street documentarians, artists who reported on life in some of the roughest and poorest ghettos in America. Unlike rap from the golden era, which tended to have an optimistic, boastful viewpoint, gangsta rap was confrontational and even threatening to some listeners.

Gangsta rap featured violent lyrics along with sexually explicit themes that many critics and activists labeled as demeaning to women. It created a firestorm of controversy that led to courtroom battles and boycotts. The more explicit the material, the more attention it received.

Schoolly D Paves the Way

Inspired by the gritty raps of Mele Mel on "The Message," aspiring Philadelphia rapper Schoolly D decided in the mid-1980s to take a similarly harsh approach with his music. Schoolly D made the first gangsta rap songs, which were profanity-filled selections in which he rapped about smoking marijuana and carrying and using guns.

At this time, rap was still in its developing stages, and record companies were unsure of the genre's potential to sell enough units to make releasing rap albums worthwhile. Schoolly D recalled that no record companies were interested in his early music:

I made one pressing ... and I took it to a disc jockey by the name of Lady B. She told me that no record company was going to sign it because I was talking about weed [marijuana] and guns ... So I thought that if [rap businessman] Russell Simmons was a rapper, he'd do his own label ... So I just said, "[I'll do it myself]." They didn't even want to hear clean rap, so I just started ... to press up my own records. I was part of a [local rap] crew anyway, so I knew everybody in every [Philadelphia record] shop, like Funk of Martin, Sound of Market. All the record stores said that if I pressed the record up, they'd sell them. So I did it.[17]

Launched in 1983, Schoolly D Records was the first artist-owned rap label. In the next few years, Schoolly D enjoyed regional, but not national, success. His hits included the thunderous "P.S.K. 'What Does It Mean?'" about his Philadelphia gang of violent friends and the story-driven "Saturday Night" about his wild adventures on Saturday nights. After Schoolly D became an underground sensation, Jive Records signed him to a recording contract and released several of his albums.

As Schoolly D was becoming one of the most talked-about rappers in the streets of Philadelphia,

Schoolly D paved the way for gangsta rappers.

INTRODUCTION OF GANGSTA RAP

COPYRIGHT INFRINGEMENT LAWSUITS

The media hype surrounding the violent lyrics of gangsta rappers and sexually explicit raps of 2 Live Crew made rap a magnet for controversy, thereby exposing the music to more listeners, some of whom purchased the music simply out of curiosity. However, some of these new consumers, many of whom were older and had grown up listening to rock and roll, included listeners who had one purpose while listening to rap music: to find illegal samples contained in songs.

Sampling was a simple procedure for rap producers as soon as the practice was popularized in the mid-1980s. However, since sampling required using other people's music, it made rappers easy targets for copyright infringement lawsuits by the owners of the songs that were being sampled.

The group 2 Live Crew was targeted because of the graphic sexual content of their breakthrough 1989 album, *As Nasty as They Wanna Be*. They were sued by the estate of Roy Orbison over the group's usage of the music of the rock icon's song "Pretty Woman." Biz Markie, a successful, lighthearted rapper, saw his career grind to a near halt in 1991 when he was sued for sampling Gilbert O'Sullivan's "Alone Again Naturally" without permission. Biz's *I Need a Haircut* album was subsequently pulled from record stores, letting producers know that they faced a lawsuit if they sampled a song without first getting permission.

rappers from other cities started making equally controversial and abrasive music. Oakland, California, rapper Too $hort reported on the lifestyle of pimps and sex workers over slow, bass-heavy music; Los Angeles rappers Ice-T and Toddy Tee rapped about the violent, gang-infested streets of their city over spare beats; and the Houston, Texas, collective Geto Boys brought vivid violence to the forefront with their aggressive productions. In New York, rapper Just-Ice and rap duo Boogie Down Productions were also releasing music with violent overtones that included explicit lyrics about sex and drugs.

Straight Outta Compton

As gangsta rap was gaining momentum, Eazy-E and N.W.A appeared with music that would electrify the rap world. Eric "Eazy-E" Wright was a small-time drug dealer and aspiring record executive who revolutionized both the rap record business and the lyrical direction of the music with releases from his record company, whose roster included Eazy-E himself and his flagship group N.W.A, whose other members were Dr. Dre, Ice Cube, MC Ren, and DJ Yella.

The first Eazy-E album, *Eazy-Duz-It*, and the first N.W.A album, *Straight Outta Compton*, both released in 1988, were full of profanity and got virtually no radio or video play. With violent, jarring music that contained an unprecedented combination of humor, misogyny, and political insight, N.W.A rapped in explicit and articulate terms about the violence and drugs consuming their California communities. According to the *Washington Post*, "they weren't the first rappers to do songs about crime, guns and gang violence, but they heightened the mayhem and the profanity to an unprecedented, nearly surreal degree."[18]

As exciting as their music may have been, N.W.A also made enemies by calling out the police for abusing innocent blacks in the ghetto on *Straight Outta Compton*. Law enforcement officials did not appreciate the hostile material. In 1989, N.W.A received a now-famous letter from the Federal Bureau of Investigation (FBI) warning the group against releasing songs that advocated violence against law enforcement, while a number of police organizations decided not to provide security at N.W.A performances. The members of N.W.A were arrested and later acquitted, or found not guilty, of disorderly conduct charges in Cincinnati, Ohio, because of a song with explicit lyrics that they performed. Additionally, they had their albums seized in England because they were deemed obscene.

The controversy, along with a string of brilliant but brutal albums, drew fans to the music of Eazy-E and N.W.A, which was more polished and accessible than that of earlier gangsta rappers thanks to the crisp, driving production from Dr. Dre and DJ Yella. Their violent music and public appearances catapulted Eazy-E and N.W.A to rap superstardom. In 2015, the movie *Straight Outta Compton*, which detailed the gangsta rap group's controversial career, was released.

The Geto Boys was another gangsta rap act that was targeted because of their violent lyrics. The release of the Houston group's self-titled 1990 album was delayed when Geffen Records decided not to distribute the record, claiming it glamorized violence and graphic sexual imagery. Soon after, Geffen Records terminated its agreement with subsidiary Def American Records, which had signed the Geto Boys, citing a growing difference in creative philosophy.

In addition to enduring the wrath of law enforcement agencies and record labels unwilling to release potentially controversial material, gangsta rappers found

N.W.A was known for their explicit lyrics.

themselves under attack from journalists, who criticized the celebratory, one-sided view of violence that gangsta rap portrayed. In an article for the *Washington Post*, the late David Mills explained how the music of gangsta rappers failed to provide an even, realistic portrayal of violence in the streets:

> The hard-core street rappers defend their violent lyrics as a reflection of "reality." But for all the gunshots they mix into their music, rappers rarely try to dramatize that reality—a young man flat on the ground, a knot of lead in his chest, pleading as death slowly takes him in. It's easier for them to imagine themselves pulling the trigger.[19]

Other writers noted that the animosity toward women and the rationale for the violence depicted in the lyrics of gangsta rap songs were becoming increasingly sensational and without political overtones. Former *Baltimore Sun* pop music critic J. D. Considine wrote, "It's hard to excuse raps that present women not as people but as [objects], that offer gunplay and physical violence not as a fact of life but as a viable means of settling scores, and that suggest that attitude is a reasonable compensation for a sense of self-worth."[20]

Activism Through Gangsta Rap

One of the most common accusations leveled at gangsta rap was that it would encourage people to commit violence. Rappers did not agree, arguing instead that their music was an important expression of pain and outrage. "A record can't make nobody do anything," N.W.A's MC Ren told *Newsweek* in 1991. "Sometimes doing a record is just my way of getting back, 'cause when [police] got you jacked up on a car, and they got a gun to your head, you can't say [anything]. Doing records I can speak out. When people listen to the record, that's their way of speaking back."[21]

Another rapper who spoke out through his music was Ice Cube, who left N.W.A and started a solo career in 1990. His work often depicted the pain caused by society's seeming indifference to the suffering of blacks in ghettos across America. In his review of Ice Cube's *AmeriKKKa's Most Wanted*, the *Washington Post*'s David Mills noted, "After the mad burst of gunshots in the one-minute drama 'The Drive-By,' the voice of a newscaster is heard: 'Outside the South-Central area, few cared about the violence because it didn't affect them.' Ice Cube clearly wants to be more than scandalous."[22]

As time went on and the shock value of gangsta rap began to fade, more people began to understand the political messages sometimes contained in the music. In fact, some music critics began to write about the prophetic properties of gangsta rap. Several critics noticed that the rage and sense of injustice contained in the work of N.W.A foretold the riots that ensued after four white police officers were acquitted in the videotaped beating of black Los Angeles motorist Rodney King. *Washington Post* staff writer Richard Harrington, for instance, wrote, "In the wake of the Los Angeles riots, the media belatedly recognized that rap, in the tradition of vanguard [trailblazing] political art, had for several years provided an early warning system that didn't wake up a slumbering and inattentive bureaucracy until it was too late."[23]

LL Cool J, one the most respected members of the hip-hop community, also recognized the significance of gangsta rappers:

I listen to politicians and activists blame rap for everything under the sun, from world violence to world hunger. But if you removed every rapper from the face of the earth, you'd still have violence and wars. In fact, if not for certain rappers, "mainstream" society would have no idea of what is going on in our communities, where real war is being waged every day. For many Americans, life is rough, and gangsta rap was born out of that misery, pain, and hunger. It didn't create it.[24]

California Rap Groups

However, gangsta rap did create something significant: a new business opportunity for gangsta rappers. The success of Eazy-E and N.W.A had record labels scrambling to find their own gangsta rappers and led to a wave of artists from Compton, the tough California city that N.W.A put on the national radar. After N.W.A came Compton acts DJ Quik and Compton's Most Wanted.

A multitude of other talented, gangster-inspired rap groups from Los Angeles, including the smooth Above the Law, the political WC and the Maad Circle, and the pro-marijuana Cypress Hill, soon became hugely successful as they focused on the harsh reality that ghetto residents often faced. Suddenly, profanity, violence, and sexual content were what the record companies were looking for, which helped make gangsta rap the most popular and promoted style of rap.

Despite this new wave of California gangsta rap acts being celebrated by rap fans, critics viewed the groups as exploitative. "One group dares to call itself Compton's Most Wanted, capitalizing on that area's reputation for gang violence, a reputation made international by N.W.A's platinum album [*Straight Outta Compton*],"[25] Mills wrote.

Gangsta Rap Evolves

The tension that gangsta rap depicted soon appeared within gangsta rap groups themselves. Ice Cube left N.W.A in 1989 because of a financial dispute. Dr. Dre later departed N.W.A, also over money issues. In early 1992, Dr. Dre released "Deep Cover," a single from the soundtrack of the movie of the same name that introduced new Dr. Dre protégé Snoop Doggy Dogg, who also rapped on the song.

Snoop Doggy Dogg (known today as Snoop Dogg) was a lanky, laid-back rapper from the Los Angeles suburb of Long Beach. His slick raps and relaxed rhyme style struck a chord with rap fans. The release of "Deep Cover" established Snoop Dogg as a promising new talent and signaled the triumphant return of Dr. Dre. However, it was the release of the first Dr. Dre solo album, *The Chronic*, at the end of 1992 that made both Dr. Dre and Snoop Dogg, who was featured prominently on the album, superstars.

Whereas the music Dr. Dre produced for N.W.A is simmering with rage, the music on *The Chronic* contains a heavy funk influence, which results in a more relaxed musical sound that is easier for a wider range of people to listen to. Still, however, the lyrics written by Dr. Dre, Snoop Dogg, and other guests, including future rap stars Kurupt and Daz Dillinger, contain the same type of violent imagery and profanity that just a few years before had bothered governmental agencies, music critics, and fans.

Thanks in part to the censorship battles and critical backlash N.W.A and the Geto Boys faced, Dr. Dre and *The Chronic* were not met with the kind of heated, repeated protests that earlier gangsta rap was. Those battles had already run their course, clearing the way for mainstream outlets such as *Rolling Stone* magazine and MTV to embrace gangsta rap as a form of legitimate music. In 1997, music critic Lorraine Ali wrote in *Rolling Stone* magazine, "*The Chronic* changed the sound of hip-hop and R&B, and its effects, both positive and negative, resonate through '90s pop culture."[26] In fact, in 2011, *Rolling Stone* listed *The Chronic* on their "100 Best Albums of the '90s" list, putting it at the number 2 position.

This acceptance was a turning point for rap. For the first time, rap music commanded attention because of the quality of the music and not because it was a fad, a gimmick, or something controversial.

Challenging Free Speech

While N.W.A, Snoop Dogg, the Geto Boys, and other rap groups took violence as their theme, 2 Live Crew created controversy by creating sexually explicit material. In 1990, the Miami, Florida, rap group's third album, *As Nasty as They Wanna Be*, was pulled from record store shelves in several states, including Florida and Maryland, after government officials asked retailers to restrict sales of the album to adults. Some record stores then went a step further by removing all 2 Live Crew

FEMALE EMPOWERMENT IN RAP

Rap is typically not the first genre of music one thinks of when it comes to female empowerment, especially due to the overload of anti-women lyrics within many rappers' songs, which is one of the reasons why rap sometimes gets a bad reputation. However, there have been female and male rappers throughout rap's history who have stood up for women's rights in their music, one of the first groups being Salt-N-Pepa. They blazed the trail with several of their tracks that were focused on gender equality and female pride.

Lauryn Hill, who began her hip-hop music career with the Fugees in the early 1990s, later released her solo album *The Miseducation of Lauryn Hill* in 1998. This album touched on her pregnancy, religious faith, and falling out with the Fugees, but most importantly, it also gave an honest and realistic presentation of a black woman's view of life, love, and sexuality. In 1999, Hill won five Grammys, one of them being Album of the Year, making it the first hip-hop album to ever receive that award. In early 2018, she announced she was touring to celebrate the 20th anniversary of the album.

TLC, a female hip-hop trio consisting of Tionne "T-Boz" Watkins, Rozonda "Chilli" Thomas, and the late rapper Lisa "Left Eye" Lopes, was popular in the 1990s, having sold more than 65 million records worldwide. Their 1995 song "Waterfalls" tackled the issues of drugs and cheating, and became the first song to reach number 1 that referenced acquired immunodeficiency syndrome (AIDS). In the music video for their 1999 track "Unpretty," women consider plastic surgery and think about other body image issues; however, ultimately they overcome their insecurities with unrealistic

recordings from their stores.

In June 1990, a U.S. District Court judge in Florida ruled that *As Nasty as They Wanna Be* was obscene, and three of the four members of 2 Live Crew were arrested after performing songs that were determined to be obscene. However, in October 1990, a Florida jury, claiming to view the lyrics as art, acquitted 2 Live Crew of performing obscene material. The case drew national attention to the legal debate about freedom of speech and the difficulty of defining what is and is not obscene.

National publications covered the 2 Live Crew obscenity trial, and once it was over, some people defended the group's music. "Clearly this judgment should serve as notice to others trying to find music obscene that Americans believe very strongly in our First Amendment rights," Trish Heimers, who spoke on behalf of beauty standards so often pushed by the media.

Male rappers with female empowerment songs include Mos Def and Talib Kweli as the hip-hop duo Black Star. They released their 1998 track "Brown Skin Lady," which shows love, respect, and honor for black women, encouraging them to have pride and love for themselves.

Another example is Beastie Boys' Adam Yauch, otherwise known as MCA, who rapped in their 1994 song "Sure Shot": "I want to say a little something that's long overdue / The disrespect to women has got to be through / To all the mothers and the sisters and the wives and friends / I want to offer my love and respect to the end."[1]

1. Quoted in Jasmine Grant, "15 Feminist Rap Lyrics That Will Empower, Educate + Inspire You," VH1, March 15, 2016. www.vh1.com/news/250872/feminist-hip-hop-lyrics/.

TLC was an all-female hip-hop group who encouraged female empowerment through their lyrics.

the Recording Industry Association of America (RIAA), told the *Washington Post*. "Whether they find it vulgar or obnoxious or lewd still does not mean that it is criminally obscene."[27] Other commentators, however, took a harsher view. Former *Washington Post* columnist Jonathan Yardley wrote,

> The recording is filth, pure and simple, utterly devoid of socially or artistically redeeming qualities. "As Nasty as They Wanna Be" is to all intents and purposes one uninterrupted barrage [outpouring] of lewd and [obscene] language, a monotonous recitation of all the standard-issue four-letter words and numerous others of greater length; it is—yes—witless, [harsh], insulting to even the dullest intelligence and, above all else, contemptuous [to feel or express deep hatred] of women.

INTRODUCTION OF GANGSTA RAP 51

One of the first rap groups to challenge free speech with their explicit lyrics was 2 Live Crew.

It is beyond the powers of my imagination to conceive that it could bring pleasure to anyone, though apparently it does.[28]

Rap Rivalry

N.W.A, 2 Live Crew, and Dr. Dre earned as much media exposure as rap had ever experienced to this point, if not more, yet the rest of the rap community was not necessarily happy about the rise of the gangsta rap scene, especially in Los Angeles. New York rappers initially dismissed the gangsta rap of the West Coast as unimaginative, pointless, and not "real" hip-hop because it lacked the lyrical complexity that had blossomed during the golden era of rap. New York rapper Tim Dog even recorded a song criticizing the entire city of Compton and dedicated his debut

HIP-HOP: A CULTURAL AND MUSICAL REVOLUTION

album, 1991's *Penicillin on Wax*, to attacking the artistic merit of Los Angeles–based rappers.

West Coast rappers, such as Eazy-E, Dr. Dre, and Snoop Dogg became more popular than any other rap acts during this time. Their style influenced a legion of New York rappers, including Kool G. Rap & DJ Polo, the Beatnuts, Mobb Deep, and Fat Joe, all of whom infused their music with a gritty feel that showed the direct influence of the confrontational material of Eazy-E and N.W.A. The East Coast's distaste for West Coast rap continued, and the West Coast did not appreciate this lack of respect from the East Coast. This led to competition between the two regions, which led to rap being handled more like a business.

CHAPTER FIVE

The Rap Business Expands

As rap gained more recognition in the early 1990s, while it became more controversial and violent, it also started to create a new generation of rappers, who not only cared about the music-making aspects, but the business side as well. Rappers such as Master P, JAY-Z, Sean "Diddy" Combs, and Dr. Dre began investing their money wisely and were some of the first to create lucrative opportunities for themselves in the rap world. Many of them started their own record companies and had the power to sign artists and dictate how money was going to be spent to promote them, making rap's financial stakes bigger than ever.

Eazy-E Revamps the Rap Business Model

Like Schoolly D before him, Eazy-E decided to start his own record company, called Ruthless Records, in the 1980s. Ruthless Records released a few singles through local record distributors and enjoyed modest success, but Eazy-E wanted national exposure. A visionary who dreamed of becoming a powerful person in the music industry, he had no interest in running a record company whose artists were popular only in Southern California. He and his manager started shopping his music and that of N.W.A to major record labels.

Eazy-E was rejected by several of these labels, which were not interested in doing business with an unproven rap record executive. However, Priority Records, an independent company that had released a number of rap compilations, was interested in the graphic, shocking music that Eazy-E and N.W.A recorded. So, at a time when no rap artist from the West Coast had made a national impact, Ruthless Records signed a production deal with Priority Records for albums from these rappers. Ruthless had to deliver albums from N.W.A and Eazy-E, and Priority was

Eazy-E had a signature style that many young people tried to copy.

Los Angeles Raiders and Los Angeles Kings sports teams. Eazy-E and Ice Cube also wore Jheri curls, a hairstyle popular among black men in Los Angeles that was identified by loose curls that had a shiny appearance. Like Run-DMC before them, N.W.A inspired a generation of kids to follow their fashion lead. Los Angeles radio personality Julio G explained the appeal of Eazy-E:

He was really that street person that people relate to because everybody knows a guy like him. In the hood, everybody knows that dude. Even when you look at his pictures, it just signifies and shows you a lifestyle and an era of Los Angeles that he represented. He represented a lot of people that were like that with the Jheri curl and the hat.[29]

responsible for the distribution of those records and handling Ruthless' marketing plan, which included pushing potentially explicit themes.

The rest of the imagery N.W.A used was equally important, as it created a style that was easily identified as that of West Coast rappers. The members of N.W.A often wore dark sunglasses and all-black clothing featuring the logos of the

Even though Ruthless and Priority Records had little music industry pull, once Eazy-E and N.W.A were promoted nationally, both their music and their look became wildly popular. Eazy-E's

THE RAP BUSINESS EXPANDS | 55

Eazy-Duz-It and N.W.A's *Straight Outta Compton* sold more than 1 million copies each. At the time, that was an astronomically high figure for an independently released rap album.

Ruthless Sets the Tone

Virtually overnight, rappers became more than artists: They became businessmen who controlled the direction and vision of the music and the artists who recorded for their companies. "What Rosa Parks did for the civil rights movement, Eazy-E did for hip-hop," said Phyllis Pollack, a publicist who represented Eazy-E and some of the artists at Ruthless Records. "He kicked the door open. I know right now everybody claims to have a label, but Eric was the first hip-hop artist to really make this work on the level that he did."[30]

Rap artists, often looked down upon by corporations and executives who did not view rap as music, could now put their records out themselves, market themselves as they saw fit, and still sell millions of copies, as Eazy-E had demonstrated. "He made a mark and set a blueprint for people to follow in the business," said Eazy-E's widow, Tomica Wright, who runs Ruthless Records as of 2018. "He took something that was looked upon in a negative sense, invested money in the idea and brought it to where people paid attention and wanted to listen to what he and his [artists] had to say."[31]

The success of the Eazy-E and N.W.A albums changed the music community's mind, and Eazy-E soon signed distribution deals for his other artists with a variety of record companies, including major labels Atlantic and Epic. The success of Ruthless Records made an impression on a generation of future rappers, such as the Grammy Award-winning rap group Bone Thugs-N-Harmony. The group started their own label BTNH Worldwide. Bone Thugs-N-Harmony member Layzie Bone recalled:

He showed us that you can be more than just a rapper. If it wasn't for Eazy-E, there probably wouldn't have been any Master Ps [the rapper whose No Limit Records was among the most successful rap record companies in the late 1990s] or Roc-A-Fellas [the company co-founded by JAY-Z]. All of them are patterned off of what Eazy-E did. He showed them everything, how to own your masters, be in control of your company and get the bulk of your money.[32]

Rappers in Movies

Some rappers began appearing in movies or commercials. This was widely seen as selling out in the first decade or so of recorded rap music,

Will Smith (right) became a major player in rap music, television, and film.

as the movies and commercials of that time typically cast rappers in shallow, stereotypical roles. However, both business-minded rappers looking to increase their exposure (and bank accounts) and movie studios looking for new ways to attract people to movie theaters realized in the early 1990s that rappers could be major box office draws.

Almost a decade after the release of such rap-inclusive films as *Flashdance* and *Breakin'*, the movie studios started casting rappers, most of whom had no formal acting training or experience, in leading roles for major motion pictures. Most of these films and television programs featured rappers in roles that required little acting and for the most part mirrored their rapping personas. Lighthearted duo

THE RAP BUSINESS EXPANDS   57

Kid 'n Play launched the successful *House Party* franchise in 1990. Ice-T, who appeared in *Breakin'* in 1984, scored a starring role as a police officer in *New Jack City*, an acclaimed film that also features cameos from hip-hop figures such as Flavor Flav and Fab 5 Freddy. Ice-T later went on to be a main cast member of *Law & Order: Special Victims Unit*, joining the cast in 2000. As of 2018, he is still on the TV show. Ice Cube also made a successful transition into film with the acclaimed film *Boyz n the Hood* in 1991.

Will Smith, better known then by his rap name the Fresh Prince, became a television star in 1990 thanks to his leading role in *The Fresh Prince of Bel-Air*. In the show, Smith played a fun-loving, mischievous teen who moves to the wealthy Los Angeles suburb of Bel-Air to avoid the pitfalls and temptations of his native Philadelphia streets. Smith, however, took a major gamble in 1993 when he portrayed a gay hustler who befriends a rich white couple in the movie *Six Degrees of Separation*. The impressive performance helped establish Smith as a credible actor who was eventually nominated for major film awards. Some of Smith's most memorable movies include the 1996 action blockbuster *Independence Day*, the *Men in Black* franchise, and 2016's *Suicide Squad*. In 2017, it was announced Smith would be portraying the Genie in the 2019 live-action remake of Disney's *Aladdin*.

Death Row Records

With many rappers selling millions of albums with their own

Snoop Dogg released his first album Doggystyle *in 1993.*

HIP-HOP: A CULTURAL AND MUSICAL REVOLUTION

companies and others gradually becoming box office stars, the stage was set for a rap company to become one of the most dominant forces in the popular music business. The creative force behind this new company already had a history of making provocative, popular music.

In 1991, bodyguard and aspiring music industry mogul Marion "Suge" Knight, reportedly through threats of violence, got Dr. Dre out of his recording contract with Ruthless Records. Knight and Dr. Dre formed their own company, Death Row Records, which released Dr. Dre's solo album, *The Chronic*, in 1992.

The success of the album established Death Row Records as one of the most powerful rap record companies in the country. Death Row Records' next release was *Doggystyle*, the first album from Snoop Dogg. It debuted as the top album in the country upon its release in 1993, making Snoop Dogg the first new artist ever to have an album enter the pop music charts at number 1. After fewer than two years in business, Death Row Records thus had the respect of the music industry and the best-selling album in the nation.

Bad Boy Entertainment

While Death Row Records was dominating the rap market, New Yorker Sean "Diddy" Combs was making plans to enter the rap world as a label head, too. An established music producer, Combs formed Bad Boy Entertainment in 1993 and landed a distribution deal with industry powerhouse Arista Records. The deal ensured that all Bad Boy releases would be available at record stores worldwide.

The next year, Bad Boy Entertainment became an industry powerhouse itself when it released the epic 1994 debut album *Ready to Die* by The Notorious B.I.G., formerly known as Biggie Smalls, the stocky Brooklynite who possessed tremendous rapping skills. His wordplay was witty, his vocabulary was large, his delivery was flawless, his timing was perfect, his voice was commanding, and his song concepts were innovative. *Ready to Die* made perfect use of all of these talents and gave New Yorkers a gangsta rapper from their own area to support.

Equally important was that *Ready to Die* was a New York (or East Coast) interpretation of gangsta rap. Unlike most East Coast rappers before him, B.I.G. infused his music with the edge, paranoia, and rage that filled the best gangsta rap albums. As a storyteller, B.I.G. depicted himself in a variety of dangerous situations, making his album a journey through the New York rap underworld, just as

THE RAP BUSINESS EXPANDS

The Notorious B.I.G. was known for his witty delivery of clever lyrics.

Eazy-E and N.W.A had taken listeners on similar trips through Los Angeles a few years earlier.

In "Warning," for example, B.I.G. raps about being hunted down for his wealth, while on "Gimme the Loot" he is the one doing the robbing. "Juicy" documents his rise from average ghetto resident to hip-hop star. On "Big Poppa," B.I.G. raps over a smooth, keyboard-driven beat that has the same slow, relaxed feel of much of the Los Angeles rap of the time. By contrast, New York rap generally featured heavy drum patterns, boastful rhymes, and aggressive delivery styles.

Death Row and Bad Boy Rivalry

The differences between New York and Los Angeles rap became a point of disagreement among rap fans. Furthermore, with rap releases now regularly debuting as the number-1 album in the country and rap albums routinely selling millions of copies, rap became a crucial focus of the media. To many of those in the rap community, the attention meant that the stakes were higher and that they would do whatever was necessary to be considered the best. Rap had become more than just music or a way for people to express themselves. It was now big business, requiring a constant struggle by the artists and the companies to which they were signed to keep delivering.

The two rap labels earning most of the accolades during this period were Death Row Records and Bad Boy Entertainment. In 1995, a rivalry between the two companies—and eventually between the West Coast and East Coast styles of rap—was officially born.

At the Source Awards, an event held in New York by the industry-leading publication to celebrate rap, Death Row's Suge Knight addressed the audience, several of whom were rap artists. He urged rappers and singers who did not want company chief executive officers (CEOs) appearing on their songs and in their videos to sign with Death Row Records. The comments were aimed at Bad Boy's Diddy, who was getting a reputation for appearing on songs and in videos of his artists. Diddy was criticized for this because it appeared as though he was trying to steal the spotlight for himself. When he appeared onstage later in the show, Diddy downplayed any animosity Knight intended. Nonetheless, in a show of support for the East Coast, the New York crowd later booed Death Row's Snoop Dogg, who felt disrespected by the outpouring of hostility. The fallout from this event led to a deadly rap rivalry.

2Pac Added to Death Row Records

West Coast rapper 2Pac was added to the Death Row Records roster in 1995. Before signing, he had released three hit albums, delivered acclaimed appearances in a number of films, and was serving time in prison for sexual assault (sexual behavior or contact that occurs without the victim's consent). Eager to regain his freedom, the rapper agreed to sign with Death Row Records if it would speed up his release from prison. Death Row obliged, and overnight, 2Pac became the star of the label.

One year before this, 2Pac was shot five times (and survived) in an apparent robbery attempt in the lobby of Times Square's Quad Recording Studios in New York. In a series of interviews with the national media, he accused both Diddy and The Notorious B.I.G. of involvement in the shooting. His accusations further strained the already fragile relationship between Bad Boy and Death Row artists and established 2Pac as a star who was willing to speak his mind, regardless of whom he might offend.

Like his public statements, 2Pac's music was equally noteworthy. During his raps, he displayed several emotions and offered up thoughtful reflections. He was a performer who many fans could identify with because of his willingness to share his pain and confusion. He did not put himself above his listeners. Instead, he was just like them, struggling to find his way in an increasingly complicated world. Young Noble, a friend of 2Pac's and a member of the rap group Outlawz, explained how he and his group have been influenced by 2Pac:

> He was our teacher as far as all this [the music business]. We watched him. We'd be on the way to the studio and there'd be something that would happen and he's putting it in a rap, right there on the spot. To me, that's what music is about, experience. When you make music like that, it lasts forever. That's why some people would rather listen to some oldies than what's out now. It's timeless when it comes from the heart if you do it right.[33]

As important as 2Pac's music was, he also changed rap in other ways. Through his aggressive videos, 2Pac became the model image for what a rapper was supposed to

2Pac—also known as Tupac—is one of the most famous names from this period in rap history.

HIP-HOP: A CULTURAL AND MUSICAL REVOLUTION

UNSOLVED: THE MURDERS OF TUPAC AND THE NOTORIOUS B.I.G.

In February 2018, USA Network released *Unsolved: The Murders of Tupac and The Notorious B.I.G.* The series follows the tragic murders of the two competing legendary rap superstars. The 10 episodes take an in-depth look inside the police investigations of Detective Greg Kading (played by Josh Duhamel) and Detective Russell Poole (played by Jimmi Simpson). Tupac Shakur and The Notorious B.I.G. are portrayed by Marcc Rose and Wavyy Jonez, respectively. Rose previously played the role of Shakur in 2015's *Straight Outta Compton*, a biopic about the career of rap group N.W.A. Jonez, who wants to be a hip-hop artist, was thrilled to get the chance to play B.I.G. and explained how the series showed the two rappers in a different light than they are normally depicted in:

> Often people leave that [the rappers were close] out because they broadcast the whole 'east coast/west coast' rivalry. So for us to have the opportunity to bring life to that, and for people to be able to see that on screen, that these two were actually friends, it means a lot to me and I'm sure it means a lot to a lot of hip-hop fans and family and friends who actually knew these fellas.[1]

1. Quoted in Mike Bloom, "Marcc Rose and Wavyy Jonez Talk Playing Rap Legends in *Unsolved: The Murders Of Tupac And The Notorious B.I.G.*," *Parade*, February 27, 2018. parade.com/648176/mikebloom/marcc-rose-and-wavyy-jonez-talk-playing-rap-legends-in-unsolved-the-murders-of-tupac-and-the-notorious-b-i-g/.

act and look like. That image included acting like a thug (a term 2Pac applied to himself) and wearing bandannas—something Los Angeles gang members were also famous for doing.

Already upset with The Notorious B.I.G. and Diddy, 2Pac was more than happy to oblige when Suge Knight asked him to put down both B.I.G. and Diddy at every opportunity. This allowed him to release the rage he felt toward them, and it also earned him millions of fans.

Demise of Rap's Heavyweights

In December of 1995, 2Pac released the single "California Love," a duet with Dr. Dre that marked 2Pac's first release on Death Row Records. The song quickly became the biggest rap song of the season and set the stage for the February 1996 release of his first Death Row Records release, the double album *All Eyez on Me*.

However, it was the 2Pac single "Hit 'Em Up" that had music fans in a frenzy. In this

THE RAP BUSINESS EXPANDS

confrontational tune, 2Pac levels harsh insults at B.I.G. and the rest of the Bad Boy roster. The Outlawz also appeared in this song and proceeded to vocally pummel B.I.G. and his crew. "Hit 'Em Up" stands as one of the most stinging songs in rap history.

While Death Row became more popular and embraced violence, it lost its creative musical edge. Dr. Dre, for one, did not condone the increasingly hostile Death Row environment and later in 1996 left the label he had cofounded. However, 2Pac was not able to leave the label on his own terms. At the peak of his rivalry with B.I.G. and Bad Boy, 2Pac was shot and killed in Las Vegas, Nevada, in September 1996. The murder remains unsolved. Six months after 2Pac's death, The Notorious B.I.G. was shot to death in Los Angeles.

After the deaths of two of rap's most beloved artists, the hip-hop industry went through a transformation. The violence in gangsta rap lyrics had gone beyond the music and was acted out in real life. These tragedies caused a dip in the success of rap on the East Coast and West Coast. However, rappers from other regions of the country were refining their craft, in hopes of becoming rap's next big thing.

CHAPTER SIX

Southern Rap and
the Reemergence of DJs

In the spring of 1997, after the loss of two of gangsta rap's biggest stars—2Pac and The Notorious B.I.G.—the genre had earned a bad reputation, which caused hesitation from record companies to sign these kinds of artists. Instead they aimed to sign safer, less confrontational artists, which led to a new focus on two other groups of hip-hoppers: southern rappers and DJs.

Both rappers and DJs from the South and Midwest had been marginalized by other rappers, DJs, and major recording companies in New York and Los Angeles. Nonetheless, they had developed their own followings, with different levels of success. The South became the hottest breeding ground for rap in the mid- to-late 1990s, while DJs developed a sizable following for their own work.

Southern and Midwestern Rap

As rap emerged as a cultural power, more people wanted to participate. For a three- to four-year period beginning in about 1995, artists with divergent sounds and lyrical approaches started making rap music in such cities as Atlanta, Georgia; Memphis, Tennessee; Houston, Texas; and New Orleans, Louisiana. In each city, a specific and identifiable sound emerged that was distinguishable from the rap music coming from other cities. These distinguishing sounds led to an increasing regionalism in rap, as many fans stopped listening to music from other areas and supported artists from their own city, who used the same slang and rapped about local issues that mattered to them.

For example, the southern artists in particular rhymed over either energetic beats or beats that used the same soulful feel as the music used in 1970s blaxploitation films. (These low-budget films featured predominantly black casts at a time when blacks had few roles in major motion pictures.) Southern rappers also expanded the types of deliveries that rappers employed and the nuances

OutKast was one of the first popular rap acts from the South.

of the raps themselves. OutKast, for instance, did not hide their southern twang in their raps, as other southern rappers had done before. Indeed, an important release for southern rap was *Southernplayalisticadillacmuzik*, the 1994 debut album from OutKast, the Atlanta duo consisting of André 3000 (formerly known as Dré) and Big Boi. The album resonated because for one of the first times in rap history, a rap act from the South did not copy or imitate the sound and style of established rappers from the East or West. Rather, the duo embraced their Atlanta roots, used southern slang in their raps, and rapped about the black experience in the South. Mississippi rapper David Banner recalled the impact *Southernplayalisticadillacmuzik* had on his life: "Hearing 'Southernplayalisticadillacmuzik' was literally life-changing for me ... This was the total synthesis of what I dreamed Hip Hop to be: It had the grooves, it had the aura of Hip Hop, but it came from a pure Southern perspective."[34]

Other rappers also saw the South as a fertile ground for new rap expression. Suave House, an independent Houston rap label, released hugely successful albums from 8Ball & MJG. LaFace Records, a label backed by Arista, also set up shop in Atlanta and signed OutKast and Goodie Mob.

Despite the achievement of this wave of southern artists, rappers not located in New York or Los Angeles still had a hard time getting people to take their music seriously. Chingy, a party rhymer from St. Louis, Missouri, best known for his 2003 hits "Right Thurr" and "Holidae In," explained how difficult it was for rappers from smaller cities to break through:

The challenge of that is that somebody in New York, they have big opportunities. They're around the stuff. We're not around it, so we're struggling four times as hard as them, for real. We've got to wait till somebody comes to the city or we've got to leave out the city to try to go and find people to get them to listen to our music. We don't have big record companies and all that.[35]

DIY Rappers

Their lack of connections to the music industry did not prevent rappers from the South and Midwest from using advances in recording technology to their advantage. Previously, few artists were able to use studios because they could not afford to buy and store the equipment necessary to record music. Recording equipment was typically large and heavy and required at least two large rooms to operate. However, as smaller recording equipment became available and personal computers became capable of recording and storing music, making professional-sounding music outside a studio became possible for a new generation of artists.

These rappers, eager to get their music heard, skipped the steps of recording an album and shopping a demo to a record company. Instead, they made their own albums and released the albums themselves through their own small record companies, which were typically run out of their homes. Sometimes, after creating a name for themselves by selling their albums in the streets and to select record stores, these small record companies were able to land a deal with a regional distributor.

The larger distribution ensured that the albums of southern artists were available in more than just their own cities, which leveled out the competition with East Coast and West Coast rappers. Writer Matt Miller explained how the South became prominent in the rap world, when originally it had been harder for this region to promote its rap artists due to its competition with New York and Los Angeles:

Strategically deployed, "southernness" was no longer a handicap within rap. As the acceptance of southern rappers, producers, and audiences grew, the need for the expression of ideas related explicitly to a Southern imaginary subsided. With anti-southern bias receding as a barrier to success, the Dirty South as a point of affiliation also diminished, while increased exposure of rap scenes in major southern cities created competition at a more focused level.[36]

Many Southern rappers created such a presence in their own region that the major labels signed them to recording contracts. Banner explained,

MIDWEST RAPPERS

In the mid-to-late 1990s, rappers from cities in the Midwest became respected national rap stars for the first time. Detroit, Michigan, rapper Eminem was the biggest of these artists. Backed by production from former N.W.A member Dr. Dre, Eminem made controversial statements and recorded songs that seemed to endorse violence, similar to what N.W.A had done nearly a decade before him. However, with his shocking rap style, Eminem won 15 Grammy Awards, and according to Nielsen Music, has sold more than 47.7 million albums in the United States.

In October 2017, Eminem spoke out in a video during the BET Hip-Hop Music Awards in protest against President Donald Trump with his freestyle cypher "The Storm." His ninth album, *Revival*, which also has an overtly political tone, was released in December 2017. It served as his eighth straight album to top the Billboard 200 chart, although it received several unfavorable reviews.

Another rapper who hails from the Midwest is Kanye West. The Chicago, Illinois, rapper first made hip-hop beats for artists, such as Foxy Brown, Jermaine Dupri, and Lil' Kim. However, West's big break came when he caught the eye of JAY-Z, who had West produce one-third of the tracks on his 2001 album *The Blueprint*. West went on to contribute production on many different albums, including Nas's *The Lost Tapes* and T. I.'s *Trap Muzik*. It was not until 2004 that West released his debut album, *The College Dropout*, which reflected on his life since he had gone to college for a year, then dropped out to pursue his musical aspirations.

If you look at the South, most of us didn't come from demos or having one hot verse on the mix CD. Me, Lil Jon, T. I., Ludacris—we all put out independent albums. We'd all sold hundreds of thousands of records before we got signed [to major labels]. I had more spins than 85 percent of the people that was in the urban department of Universal before I got signed to Universal. So I think that people should respect us as artists and as businessmen.[37]

Master P Means Business

One rapper who was also successful as a businessman was Master P. Born in New Orleans, the rapper relocated to Richmond, California, about 20 miles (32 km) north of San Francisco, and opened a record store, No Limit Records. Master P paid attention to what kind of rap his customers were buying and in the early 1990s decided to launch a career as a rapper on his own No Limit Records label. He noticed that rap fans still wanted to hear hard-hitting gangsta rap, even though the major

The album earned the rapper 3 Grammy Awards; as of 2018, he has 21.

Since then, West has released many more albums, which have received widespread acclaim from critics. As of 2018, he is a record-breaking artist with the most consecutive albums appearing at number 1 on the Billboard charts. In 2016, West broke another record with his seventh studio album *The Life of Pablo*. With this record, he became the first artist to go platinum from just streaming. In April 2018, he announced that in June of the same year, two more albums would be released—one with Kid Cudi and another with only seven songs.

Kanye West released his debut album in 2004.

record companies were moving away from it because of the violence associated with the genre after recent rapper deaths.

After tirelessly promoting himself and No Limit in the Bay Area and southern states such as Louisiana and Texas, Master P and other No Limit artists, including Mystikal and Silkk the Shocker, became a force in independent rap music. Rather than making harsh, mid-tempo music like many gangsta rappers before them, they rapped over up-tempo beats that were faster and more dance-friendly. Other acts, especially the popular Memphis rap acts 8Ball & MJG and Three 6 Mafia, also made this style of up-tempo gangsta rap and sold millions of albums in the late 1990s.

Crunk Music

The progression of gangsta rap into danceable music gained the most momentum in Atlanta, where a type of music called crunk—a style with aggressive production and chanting choruses—was developed.

SOUTHERN RAP AND THE REEMERGENCE OF DJS

Lil Jon & the East Side Boyz popularized what is called crunk music.

Atlanta-based Lil Jon & the East Side Boyz are the premier crunk artists. The trio emerged in 1997 with their first album, the independently released *Get Crunk, Who U Wit: Da Album*. In a 2002 interview, Lil Jon explained why Atlanta became so popular for the crunk style of rap:

> You've got so many different people from so many different areas here. You've got so many different artists that come here just to go to the studio and work … Atlanta artists, we make records straight for the clubs. If your record ain't hitting in the club, then these [people] ain't gonna buy your [music]. You got [artists] that got hot club records that aren't even on the radio that's selling a lot of records in Atlanta.[38]

Cash Money Records

While crunk was shaped by the sound Lil Jon created, rap's next movement was defined not by a sonic style, but by the artists themselves. Lil Jon produced songs for artists from New York, Los Angeles, and the South and brought his sound to artists from different regions. However, in the 1990s, New Orleans–based Cash Money Records released albums full of bouncy

TRAP MUSIC

Hip-hop music has also started other subgenres of music, the most recent being trap music. This genre emerged out of the southern hip-hop and rap scene, particularly in Atlanta, Houston, and Memphis in the 1990s. Artists such as Ghetto Mafia and Dungeon Family were some of the first to use the term "trap" to describe the sound for this type of music known for its usage of orchestra, synthesizers, and string sections with heavy 808 kick drums. Rapper T. I., who released his second studio album, titled *Trap Muzik,* in 2003, has repeatedly said he was the creator of trap music; however, he claims he has not been given proper credit for it:

> With the exception of Outkast, let me think, Goodie Mob ... with the exception of that, before I came in the game, it was Lil Jon, Outkast, Goodie Mob, okay so you had Crunk Music and you had Organized Noise. There was no such thing as Trap Musik, I created that ... I coined the term, it was [my] second album ... After that, there was an entire new genre of music created.[1]

Some of the other rappers who popularized trap music include Waka Flocka Flame, Gucci Mane, Young Jeezy, Rick Ross, Yo Gotti, and Mannie Fresh. Producers such as Lex Luger, Zaytoven, and Young Chop can also be credited in helping to promote this genre. Current prominent artists in the trap music scene include Lil Uzi Vert, Travis Scott, Future, and Migos.

1. Quoted in Rose Lilah, "T. I. Speaks On Trap Music Genre, Says He Created It," HotNewHipHop, December 18, 2012. www.hotnewhiphop.com/t-i-speaks-on-trap-music-genre-says-he-created-it-news.3805.html.

beats produced by Mannie Fresh, which featured local rappers B.G., Juvenile, Lil Wayne, and the Big Tymers. For Lil Jon, it was about being a great producer regardless of the artist. For Cash Money, it was about being a successful New Orleans–based label with local artists who helped popularize New Orleans slang in lyrics and the city's bouncy music through Mannie Fresh's production.

However, by 2006, the departure of B.G., Juvenile, and Mannie Fresh put the future of the label in question. Birdman, cofounder of Cash Money Records, however, believed in Lil Wayne and put his full support behind him. The pair released several tracks together, along with the 2006 collaboration album titled *Like Father, Like Son.* That year, Lil Wayne was given an executive role in the company and through a string of mixtapes, guest appearances, and albums during the next few years, launched Young Money Cash Money Billionaires Records (a merging

Lil Wayne started his own record label called Young Money Entertainment.

of Cash Money Records and Wayne's Young Money Entertainment imprint) and became one of rap's hottest properties. Lil Wayne also discovered Toronto, Canada, rapper-singer Drake and female New York rapper Nicki Minaj and signed them to the imprint.

Although it was groundbreaking for a southern rapper to endorse and release material by artists from other countries, let alone New York, Nicki Minaj explained that she did not believe that signing with a southern artist would hurt her career: "The New York guys, they knew who I was.

They could have reached out, so it never bothered me that I would be coming out with someone that was technically from the South. It made it to me even a more special dynamic because it was unexpected."[39]

Despite Birdman and Wayne's close relationship, in January 2015, Lil Wayne announced a $51 million lawsuit against Cash Money Records, in which he claimed Birdman was violating his contract by not releasing *Tha Carter V*. Lil Wayne wrote on Twitter at the time, "I want off this label and nothing to do with these people but unfortunately it ain't that easy ... I am a prisoner and so is my creativity."[40] He also sought to terminate his contract with the label and take his Young Money artists Nicki Minaj and Drake with him. As of 2018, the lawsuit has yet to be resolved.

Comeback of the DJ

Thanks in large part to the success of southern rap acts in the emerging club scene and the increasing presence of rap music on radio stations, DJs again became major hip-hop figures in the mid-1990s. Therefore, even as rap became more and more prominent and graffiti artists and B-boys were increasingly marginalized by mainstream society, DJs were able to develop healthy followings.

To the bigger rap movement, the DJ's main purpose was to support the rapper, if a DJ was used at all. However, a number of other developments allowed DJs to become significant fixtures in the rap scene themselves. A crop of DJs who created mixtapes, released their own albums, toured and performed with rock-and-roll groups, and appeared on television programs became increasingly popular.

History of the Mixtape

Mixtapes were around long before "Rapper's Delight" was released. In the early and mid-1970s, DJs assembled the most popular R&B, soul, funk, and disco songs and put them on cassette tapes. These were called mixtapes because the songs from various artists were mixed together. The DJs then sold the tapes at their performances and in the streets to fans, thereby earning money and recognition.

Once rap songs became popular in the early 1980s, DJs included rap songs on their mixtapes. Later in the 1980s, DJs such as Kid Capri and Ron G realized that they could also make mixtapes solely of rap songs and that those mixtapes were even more popular among their customers.

In the 1990s, mixtapes, especially those in New York, began to feature unreleased music from artists. Individual DJs tried to forge relationships with star rappers hoping they would give them a copy of new songs first. This arrangement gave such DJs as Funkmaster Flex and DJ Clue? a reputation for having the newest music and made them celebrities in their own right.

Even though rappers enjoyed the exposure their songs gained from mixtapes, many record companies disliked DJs because their mixtapes featured music that the companies did not authorize for release. DJs therefore labeled many mixtapes "for promotional use only" and did not technically offer them for sale. That way, the record companies could not sue the DJs because they could claim they were not selling the mixtapes.

DJs Showcase Their Talents

As DJs regained their status throughout the 1990s, a number of high-profile DJs graduated from releasing their own self-funded and self-distributed mixtapes to signing deals with major record companies to release albums nationally. The albums from DJs came in a variety of formats.

Pioneering mixtape DJ Kid Capri released *The Tape* in 1991. Although the album features the popular DJ rapping, it failed to gather much interest. It took several years for a mixtape DJ to get another chance to put an album out on a national level. Then popular club and radio DJ Funkmaster Flex broke through in the mid-1990s with *The Mix Tape* series of albums, which were like traditional mixtapes. The albums contain a number of classic rap songs as well as songs exclusive to the album.

DJ Clue?'s *The Professional* album, which arrived in 1998, is in the format of mixtapes. It features all original material from some of rap's hottest artists, including Missy Elliott and JAY-Z.

Another type of album put out by DJs featured them scratching over their own self-produced beats. Released by such DJs as the X-Ecutioners, these albums were showcases for the mixing, scratching, and production skills of the DJ, unlike the majority of mixtapes and albums put out by DJ Clue? and DJ Kay Slay, which featured popular rappers rather than the DJs' own turntable abilities.

Influential People in the Mixtape Business

Mixtapes and mixtape DJs remained a New York phenomenon until about 2002, when 50 Cent changed the way mixtapes were made. The rapper was released from his recording contract with major label Columbia Records when he was shot and almost killed in 2000. After recovering, 50 Cent resumed making music. Unable to get a new recording contract, 50 Cent took instrumental versions of popular songs and made his own covers of them. He then compiled the cuts with DJ Whoo Kid onto mixtapes and released them to the underground mixtape scene in New York.

The strategy paid off for 50 Cent, who featured his rhyme crew, G-Unit, on many of his mixtape releases. With his name and music gathering attention in New York and radio stations playing his mixtape songs on the radio—something that had rarely happened before—several record companies started pursuing the rapper. In 2002, 50 Cent signed to Dr. Dre's Aftermath Entertainment and Eminem's Shady Records. After selling more than 30 million copies of his own albums, 50 Cent still releases mixtapes, although less frequently than he did before signing with a major label.

The explosion of the mixtape culture, thanks in large part to the success of 50 Cent, increased the standing of DJs in the hip-hop world. In 2005, DJs such as Green Lantern and DJ Drama released mixtapes that earned as much attention as some albums. In fact, mixtape DJs are so popular and have such big

By releasing mixtapes and putting his own unique spin on them, 50 Cent became an influential person in hip-hop.

followings that many rappers give their new songs to mixtape DJs before they give them to anyone else—including their record label.

DJs Embraced by Different Outlets

As the mixtape culture developed in the late 1990s and more DJs secured major record deals, DJs became more prominent through their work independent of rappers rather than with them. Even though rappers typically distanced themselves from DJs, the DJs got a boost from a seemingly unlikely source: rock groups. Rock acts that incorporated some rapping into their work, such as Linkin Park and Kid Rock, featured DJs during their live performances. Around the same time, television shows such as *The Chris Rock Show* and *Chappelle's Show* featured DJs hired to transition the program in and out of commercial breaks. *Nick Cannon Presents: Wild 'N Out*, a sketch comedy and improvisation reality television series regularly featuring several prominent hip-hop music artists, has featured DJ D-Wrek since 2006.

From 2010 to 2013, a reality television series and DJ competition titled *Master of the Mix* aired on the BET network. The show was hosted by hip-hop record producer Just Blaze and judged by DJ Kid Capri. Many of the contestants were already experienced DJs, such as the DJs of the Rock Steady Crew and hip-hop group EPMD, who competed for the title on the show.

After being pushed to the side for quite some time as rappers enjoyed the limelight, DJs finally found their place again in the hip-hop movement. Some DJs even became internationally known, expanding hip-hop's reach to countries beyond the United States, which led to hip-hop's global explosion.

SOUTHERN RAP AND THE REEMERGENCE OF DJS

CHAPTER SEVEN

The New Global *Rap Landscape*

In the 2000s, the internet became the primary outlet to discover new rap artists who otherwise would have remained unknown. As hip-hop culture became more widespread in American society, it also expanded its reach into different countries, with each country incorporating a bit of their own cultural heritage into the movement. The genre is currently more universal than ever, and its once regional borders have fallen, making it a global influence.

While there are more hip-hop artists than ever before, there has been a transformation in the way they release their music. The days of an artist sticking to the strategic formula of putting out a lead single, announcing their album's release date, and heading out on a coinciding tour are in the past. Now with streaming services and other forms of releasing music, more artists are experimenting with the element of surprise. As the hip-hop world experiences innovation, it seems there is no stopping its ever-evolving progress.

File Sharing

In the early 2000s, as hip-hop's reach expanded throughout the business world, sales of albums throughout the music industry decreased significantly, including those of rappers. At least some of the sales decline was due to the rampant illegal downloading and file sharing of digital music on websites such as Napster and Limewire. In 2003, however, Apple's iTunes became the first music service credited with convincing people to pay for digital music again.

Furthermore, several important record store chains, including Tower Records and Virgin Megastore, closed during the 2000s, providing fewer locations for consumers to purchase music legally. All of this news was worsened by the economic recession that hit the United States in 2007, leaving many

Americans with less disposable income. In 2007, album sales dropped 9.5 percent in the United States from 2006. It was not until 2009, when the recession ended, that overall music sales, including sales of albums, singles, digital tracks, and music videos, showed a noticeable increase at $1.5 billion.

Rappers Launch Careers Online

Rap and hip-hop music has been consumed on the internet by millions of people. One rapper who capitalized on the increasing power of the internet to spread music instantly and without cost was Soulja Boy Tell 'Em, who now records as just Soulja Boy. After recording and releasing his music independently on the internet for nearly two years, Soulja Boy recorded and posted the song "Crank That (Soulja Boy)" on the internet in early 2007. Within a few months, the song became a sensation thanks to its low-budget video, which features Soulja Boy showcasing the "Crank That" dance.

Soulja Boy was known for launching his rap career online with his song "Crank That (Soulja Boy)."

THE NEW GLOBAL RAP LANDSCAPE

Prior to the time of the internet, aspiring artists would record material and offer it to record companies, established music producers, or veteran artists. These artists hoped that their music would appeal to one of the established music industry insiders, who would then sign them to a recording contract. Soulja Boy, on the other hand, skipped all the middle men by using the internet to independently release and promote his music.

Veteran rap producer Mr. ColliPark, who had worked with Ying Yang Twins and David Banner, signed the then-16-year-old Soulja Boy to a recording contract. The song "Crank That (Soulja Boy)" became a hit online, was featured on the cable television program *Entourage*, and peaked at number 1 on the Billboard Hot 100 chart.

Given the almost instant success of "Crank That (Soulja Boy)," Soulja Boy did not go through the typically long process of recording an albums' worth of material before landing a recording contract, as is the case with most artists.

Soulja Boy's rise marked a new way for artists to gain entrance to the music industry. The internet leveled the playing field for emerging rap artists by giving independent artists, who had limited financial resources to make high-budget videos or tour the country, a place to distribute their music, instantly making it accessible to anyone who wanted to listen to it. It also signaled several other shifts in how rap was being consumed and created.

Rap Loses Regionalism

One of these shifts has been in the way listeners discover new artists and songs. In the 1980s through the early part of the 2000s, music lovers encountered fresh sounds through rap videos shown on MTV, BET, and other television networks. Another way for listeners to discover new music was through radio stations. However, these outlets restricted the listeners' experience by selecting which songs and videos were played and when they were played. With the internet, these barriers no longer exist. People choose which videos they want to watch or which songs they want to listen to online without having to wait for the video to be played on television or the song to be played on the radio. Now, because of the internet, access is immediate.

When music listeners first discovered the internet, they found that they could instantly listen to music beyond just what was popular in their geographic region. For example, a New York rap fan who grew up in the 1990s and enjoyed the music of West Coast artists, such as Ice Cube and Too $hort, most likely would not have been able to hear their material on the radio because the rap music at the time tended to be region-specific. A New York radio station tended to play music from rappers from New York. In the 2000s, however, that same New York rap fan would be able to go to YouTube and a number of other websites and listen to material from Ice Cube, Too $hort, and virtually any other artist on demand. In addition to connecting listeners with artists, this shift also allowed like-minded artists to get in touch with each other more easily.

Technology Allows for Other Changes

Rappers having more exposure to artists from different regions allowed them to become more diverse as artists. It also allowed two artists to be on opposite sides of the world and still collaborate to produce a track because of the evolution of technology.

Music producers are able to email the file of a song while it is being recorded to another artist or musician anywhere in the world. The artist can then download the song, record their material, and email it back to the producer. The producer can then make the song by adding the elements from the different performers without ever having the artists together in the same studio.

Rapper The Game, for instance, received the music for the song that would eventually become "Red Nation" from his 2011 album, *The R.E.D. Album*, while on tour in Germany. The song also features Lil Wayne. The Game, the producers Cool & Dre, and Lil Wayne were not in the studio at the same time during the majority of the recording process.

Streaming Services

Another platform that made listening to music from anywhere in the world easier and increased music sales, especially for hip-hop artists, was music streaming services. These services, such as Spotify, TIDAL, Apple Music, Pandora, and Amazon Music, among others, allow users to listen to music in real time, as opposed to downloading a file onto the computer to listen to later.

These services allow users to listen to what seems like endless amounts of music for a monthly membership fee or for free depending on the service. These music platforms have helped the music industry in earning more sales, but have also assured that the artists releasing music would be properly compensated and would have more control over distribution of their content. It has also improved the listening experience for consumers, giving them more music to choose from at an affordable price.

In 2017, rapper Cardi B rose to

considerable fame once her debut single "Bodak Yellow" began streaming. It only took 6 weeks for the track to reach number 1 on Billboard's Hot Rap Songs chart, which made it the fastest debut to top that chart since PSY's 2012 viral hit "Gangnam Style." In regards to how streaming has affected the music industry, Motown Records president Ethiopia Habtemariam said, "Streaming was just a big reveal of what was already happening … [But] I don't think people were equipped to handle it. Now I see [companies] hiring a lot more people that come from the culture."[41]

Prior to streaming, a hip-hop track such as this would have either been given away as a download on mixtape sites, such as DatPiff or LiveMixtapes, or downloaded illegally in some other way in the early 2000s (meaning the artist would not properly be compensated for their music).

"We suffered from piracy, we suffered from the free model, and we weren't demanding anything in return for our art," said Ghazi Shami, owner of record label and distribution company Empire. "Now there's a new generation that says it's okay to pay a subscription fee to Apple Music or Spotify."[42]

If a track, such as "Bodak Yellow," had been purchased legally, it would have been through an online music store; however, not as many people were likely to do this without hearing the song first, which meant less sales and less people hearing the actual music.

Anthony Saleh, CEO of Emagen Entertainment Group and the manager of Nas and Future, also commented on the innovation of streaming: "Hip-hop has been this big for a long time, but now people get to see it."[43]

SoundCloud

One of the most popular streaming services for the hip-hop community is SoundCloud, which launched in 2007 and allows users around the world to listen to millions of songs or upload their own songs. The music streaming and sharing platform based in Berlin, Germany, fostered the development of what has been called "SoundCloud rap." Several rappers who got their start on SoundCloud include Lil Uzi Vert, Lil Pump, Post Malone, Travis Scott, and Lil Yachty. SoundCloud rap is characterized by its distinct sound, which is typically a mix of trap, lo-fi, electronic, and hip-hop music. Artists of this genre are also known for the short length of their songs, their popular social media presences, and sometimes their dangerous drug use, especially Xanax. The late SoundCloud rapper Lil Peep died from an accidental fentanyl and Xanax overdose in November 2017.

Early on in his career, Chance the Rapper would upload his music to SoundCloud.

In July 2017, when Chicago rapper Chance the Rapper heard SoundCloud had laid off 40 percent of their staff and was possibly shutting down, he tweeted, "I'm working on the SoundCloud thing."[44] The rapper, who stepped onto the music scene in 2011 and earned three Grammys for his third mixtape *The Coloring Book*, has often credited SoundCloud for helping him find early success. After streaming the mixtape exclusively on Apple Music on May 13, 2016, two weeks later, he streamed it on SoundCloud and distributed it to other various music streaming platforms. As the album achieved widespread praise, it became the first album to chart on the Billboard 200 solely off of streams, reaching the number 8 position. It also was the first streaming-only album to ever win a Grammy.

During his Grammy acceptance speech in February 2017, he gave a shout-out to SoundCloud: "This is for every indie artist, everybody who's been doing this mixtape stuff for a [long] time … Shouts out to DJ Drama for doing it first. You put in that time. Shouts out to every independent artist out there. Shouts out to SoundCloud for holding me down!"[45]

After speaking with SoundCloud CEO Alex Ljung, Chance the Rapper assured SoundCloud was not going to close its doors, and to help support the platform, he released the SoundCloud exclusive track "Big B's" featuring Young Thug.

Creative Marketing

Music streaming services also encouraged artists to become more creative when releasing their new albums. Instead of merely announcing an album's release date

THE NEW GLOBAL RAP LANDSCAPE

TIDAL

In January 2015, JAY-Z purchased the Sweden-based company Aspiro for $56 million. Through this purchase, he constructed and launched TIDAL—the first artist-owned digital-music streaming service. On March 30, 2015, he threw a TIDAL launch party in New York City. He was joined by some of the biggest names in the music business, and each was offered a 3 percent stake in the company upon signing on as exclusive artists. These exclusive artists would release their new music first on TIDAL and offer up other special content to subscribers. These artists included Beyoncé, Kanye West, Jack White, and Alicia Keys, among many others.

JAY-Z began TIDAL because he wanted to give some power back to the artists in the music industry while also bringing a higher quality product to consumers. Alicia Keys explained the main goal of TIDAL at the event: "Our goal is simple: We want to create a better service and a better experience for both fans and artists … We believe that it is in everyone's interests—fans, artists and the industry as a whole—to preserve the value of music, and to ensure a healthy and robust industry for years to come."[1]

1. Quoted in Todd Spangler, "Jay Z Launches Tidal Streaming-Music Service at Star-Studded Event," *Variety*, March 30, 2015. variety.com/2015/digital/news/jay-z-launches-tidal-streaming-music-service-1201462769/.

---

ahead of time, many artists have been releasing what have become known as surprise albums, such as JAY-Z's *Magna Carta… Holy Grail* in 2013 and Drake's *If You're Reading This It's Too Late* in 2015. The pre-announced release date has become "the enemy of creativity,"[46] according to Dr. Dre.

In 2017, Rick Ross did not let his record label Maybach Music Group or his distributor EPIC/Sony dictate when he would release his ninth album *Rather You Than Me*. Instead, he decided he wanted to release it on his daughter's birthday, which was March 17.

Another recent strategy some artists have implemented for releasing an album is making their music available exclusively on specific streaming services. The only early advertising JAY-Z supplied for his 13th studio album *4:44* were vague posters displayed in New York City, Los Angeles, and Miami, Florida, in June 2017. Then on June 7, a teaser was aired during the NBA Finals, ending with the message that *4:44* would be released on June 30, 2017, and would be available only on TIDAL. The rapper, who had launched TIDAL in March 2015, decided to make *4:44* available solely to TIDAL and

Sprint subscribers on June 30 for the first week, then on July 7, the album became available on other platforms. Another rap album released exclusively on TIDAL was Kanye West's seventh studio album *The Life of Pablo* on February 14, 2016. Three days before the official release, he premiered an earlier version of the album at Madison Square Garden at his Yeezy Season 3 fashion show with Adidas. Leading up to this release, there were several changes made to the title of the album. West's erratic behavior on social media regarding the album sparked many controversies, but also gained him publicity. After the album's streaming release on TIDAL, West continued to update songs on the album, which had never been done by an artist before. It was not until April 1, 2016, that an updated version of the album was released through several streaming services and for digital purchase on his official website.

Social Media's Influence on Hip-Hop

Before hip-hop artists were able to upload their music online, they relied heavily on record labels to distribute their music. Now with the innovation of streaming, many artists can take the distribution, marketing, and release of their music into their own hands—meaning they will likely see more of a profit if the release is successful rather than giving a large share of their profit to a record company.

Prior to the internet, if an up-and-coming rapper was released from their recording contract before they put out their first album, this typically would signal the end of their career. The internet, however, encouraged a do-it-yourself mentality for artists and worked in their favor. Now that rappers are able to share their music online and promote it themselves through social media outlets, such as Facebook, Twitter, and Instagram, this has altered the rap genre's model of success. Wiz Khalifa, for instance, is among a new generation of rappers who turned his newfound contractual freedom into opportunity.

Upon his release from Warner Bros. Records in 2009, Wiz Khalifa became quite productive. In less than two years, he released several mixtapes, released an independent album, and collaborated with other artists on dozens of songs. Wiz Khalifa's hard work was rewarded in 2010 with a recording contract with Atlantic Records. His single "Black and Yellow" reached the number-1 spot on Billboard's Hot 100 chart in February 2011.

In a February 2011 interview, Wiz Khalifa explained the lessons he learned when he was dropped from Warner Bros. Records: "I

Success of Foreign Hip-Hop Artists

After DJ and hip-hop pioneer Afrika Bambaataa organized the first European hip-hop tour in 1982, the rest of the world began to take notice of hip-hop culture. Over time, people in other countries embraced hip-hop, and they began developing their own subgenres of hip-hop and rap, such as trip-hop, grime, and reggaeton. As these artists were building their musical collections, however, those outside their country may not have been aware of their existence until after the rise of the internet. Once these artists were accessible to a larger audience over the web, their visibility and popularity increased.

Fans often feel a special connection with rappers from their own country, who rap in their native language about topics relevant to their homeland. Rappers around the world have taken their American predecessors' cue by using their raps to discuss political issues and express their outrage at social injustices.

After being let go by his record label, Wiz Khalifa released mixtapes independently and achieved success on his own.

basically just learned to work for myself and keep everything internal, stick with the people you've been grinding with, just to put on the home team. Stick with that and be able to present that to a label, rather than letting them determine what your marketing and stuff like that is going to be like."[47]

Hip-Hop Subgenres Overseas

In England, rap quickly developed its own scene, as London rapper Derek

84 HIP-HOP: A CULTURAL AND MUSICAL REVOLUTION

B released his album *Bullet from a Gun* in 1988 on Profile Records, also home to Run-DMC. Even though he did not become a major rap force in America, he nonetheless helped establish the London rap scene. In November 2009, he died of a heart attack in London.

Three years after Derek B brought British rap international attention, French-based rapper MC Solaar earned a worldwide following because of his nimble raps and the jazz-inspired music over which he rapped. His first album, 1991's *Qui Sème le Vent Récolte le Tempo* (*He Who Sows the Wind Gathers the Tempo*), was an early example of quality rap performed in a language other than English.

As French rap evolved, people in other countries began creating their own styles of rap, too. Reggaeton, from Puerto Rico, is a popular, typically energetic hybrid of rap and reggae, which is the indigenous music of Jamaica popularized by the laid-back "roots" style of Bob Marley and the more aggressive, rap-influenced dance-hall style of Buju Banton and Sean Paul. Hip-hop and reggaeton, which is typically performed in Spanish, share many similarities. Reggaeton is, according to popular artist Tego Calderón, "the new way the youth here in [Puerto Rico] express themselves, mainly it was a form of expression among the poor. It started out the same way as hip-hop did. Initially, it was totally underground. In a 10-year span people got used to listening to our music, and the music earned a space in radio shows."[48] Like hip-hop acts, reggaeton artists have a number of different musical styles. Calderón incorporates political messages into his material, while Daddy Yankee and Pitbull produce infectious dance music.

Another genre that developed in the 1990s was trip-hop, an English form of hip-hop characterized by a mixture of break beats and down-tempo electronic music that was popularized by artists such as Massive Attack and Tricky. Then in the 2000s, a slew of rappers, such as conversational rap group The Streets, female rapper and R&B singer Ms. Dynamite, and Dizzee Rascal (one of the first of these artists, alongside Wiley, Kano, and Lethal Bizzle), introduced a new kind of rap called grime. The genre is generally a mixture of U.K. garage, drum and bass, rap, and dance hall.

Evolution of Female Rappers

In the 1990s, numerous female rappers hit the scene, including Lil' Kim, Foxy Brown, Da Brat, Shawnna, and more. However, several of these rappers were considered hypersexual, which caused them to lose much of their popularity among fans and critics once the shock of their explicit lyrics and imagery wore off. Some of the less provocative and more rhyme-driven female rappers during this time were Amil, one of JAY-Z's protégés; Rah Digga, who was part of Busta Rhymes's Flipmode Squad; Three 6 Mafia's Gangsta Boo; Mia X, the first female to be signed to Master P's No Limit Records; Yo-Yo, one of Ice Cube's protégés; and Queen Pen, who was a featured rapper on BLACKstreet's 1996 track "No Diggity."

In the 2000s, there were not as many new female rappers introduced; however, Missy Elliott, Eve, Rapsody, Lil Mama, and M.I.A. made their marks. In the 2010s, female rappers—such as Angel Haze; Azealia Banks; Australian rapper Iggy Azalea; female trap artists, including DeJ Loaf, Rico Nasty, and Young M.A; and the two current female heavyweights, Nicki Minaj and Cardi B—were memorable additions to the rap scene. The internet, social media, and streaming helped get their music out to the masses.

As a young female rapper, Nicki Minaj, who was raised in Queens, New York, started by uploading her tracks to the social media website MySpace and sending them to various people in the music industry. She also released a few mixtapes, which she received praise for in the underground hip-hop community. However, Minaj's big break came shortly after this when she was discovered by Lil Wayne and, in 2009, signed with his Young Money Entertainment label. From there, she released successful albums, including 2010's *Pink Friday*, 2012's *Pink Friday: Roman Reloaded*, and 2014's *The Pinkprint*. She is known as a clever lyricist and has used her inventive wordplay, catchy beats, and multiple musical personas to become one of rap's most popular acts.

Cardi B is another female rapper who became wildly popular in 2017. Before becoming a rapper, she grew up the Bronx, struggled financially, and was even allegedly part of a gang. In 2013, she began posting humorous videos on her Vine and Instagram pages, which proceeded to go viral. She also appeared on the VH1 reality television series *Love & Hip-Hop: New York* from 2015 to 2017. During this time, she released two mixtapes and, in February 2017, signed to Atlantic Records. Her first single "Bodak Yellow" became an instant hit song and topped the Billboard Hot 100 in 6 weeks. She became the second female rapper, next to Lauryn Hill, to ever reach number 1 with a debut single as a solo artist. Cardi B released her debut album, *Invasion of Privacy*, on April 6, 2018, which debuted at number 1. The album received universal acclaim, and she became the fifth female

After achieving huge success from streaming her songs and releasing mixtapes, Cardi B released her debut album Invasion of Privacy *in April 2018.*

rapper to reach the top of the Billboard 200 chart.

Politically Charged Rap

In the era of America's widening political divide, several American rappers have produced albums with political messages following in the footsteps of some of rap's first superstars, such as N.W.A and Public Enemy. Artists such as Kendrick Lamar, Lupe Fiasco, Vince Staples, and Big K.R.I.T. have taken strong political stances in their music.

In 2016, Kendrick Lamar gave a fiery performance at the Grammys where he presented two songs, "The Blacker the Berry" and "Alright," from his 2015 album *To Pimp a Butterfly*. During his performance of "The Blacker the Berry," he came out in a line with other black men, all of whom wore shackles and were connected by chains. One of the lines he rapped was, "You hate my people, your plan is to terminate my culture,"[49] which is a commentary on the racism and stereotypes black people in America face.

Lamar received widespread acclaim for *To Pimp a Butterfly*. Gigwise's Will Butler labeled the album "a pantheon for racial empowerment." He also acknowledged it as a conscious hip-hop record that "will be revered not just at the top of some list at the end of the year, but in the subconscious of music fans for decades to come."[50]

Lamar's performance at the 2018 Grammys was equally as politically charged. He performed the tracks "XXX" and "DNA" from his 2017 album, *DAMN.*, which again explores racial inequality in

THE NEW GLOBAL RAP LANDSCAPE

Rapper Kendrick Lamar is known for addressing political topics in his music.

of the performance, as Lamar passionately rapped, gunshot sounds were heard, and his backup dancers appeared as if they were being shot down one by one, highlighting the themes of gun violence and police brutality in America. In a Pitchfork review of Lamar's *DAMN.*, Matthew Trammell described it as "a widescreen masterpiece of rap, full of expensive beats, furious rhymes, and peerless storytelling about Kendrick's destiny in America."[53] The importance of this album was further cemented when Lamar was awarded with a Pulitzer Prize for Music for *DAMN.* in April of 2018. In the 75-year history of the award, it is the first time a popular artist and a hip-hop artist received the award.

Hip-Hop Is Not Dead

When rapper Nas released his eighth studio album, *Hip Hop Is Dead*, in 2006, he was making a bold statement, in which he explained, "When I say 'hip-hop is dead,' basically America is dead. There is no political voice. Music is dead … Our way of thinking is dead, our commerce is dead. Everything in this society has been done. What I mean by 'hip-hop is dead' is we're at a vulnerable state … I think hip-hop could help rebuild America, once hip-hoppers own hip-hop."[54] However, according to Nielsen Music's 2017

America. The song "XXX" begins with a commentary on the discrimination of certain races in America with the lyrics, "America, God bless you if it's good to you."[51] In the middle of the performance, Lamar stopped rapping and the camera cut to comedian Dave Chappelle saying, "The only thing more frightening than watching a black man be honest in America, is being an honest black man in America."[52] At the end study, hip-hop and R&B are the most listened to genres of music, and these artists are starting to have more ownership of their music due to the innovations of the internet, social media, and streaming services.

Over the years, hip-hop has evolved—from the golden age of hip-hop to gangsta rap to southern rap to conscious hip-hop to trap music—and subgenres keep being created, making hip-hop one of the most diversified genres of music. Hip-hop promotes originality, creativity, and activism, and the artists of this genre have continued the tradition of speaking up for those who cannot speak for themselves. Their music serves a larger purpose; it encourages equality, challenges the norms of society, and convinces people to expand their minds to achieve understanding. Hip-hop is also inclusive, and now that the world has embraced it, people from all walks of life are participating. Andre Harrell, the founder of Uptown Records said, "Rich, poor, Asian, Hispanic, black, white, they're all part of the hip hop generation. Hip hop just gives everyone an opportunity. Everybody knows where it comes from, everybody loves it. And it's never going away."[55]

Notes

Chapter One:
The Emergence of Hip-Hop Culture

1. Quoted in Greg Kot, "Bambaataa: 'All Music Is Dance Music,'" *Chicago Tribune*, October 12, 2004. articles.chicagotribune.com/2004-10-12/features/0410120028_1_afrika-bambaataa-electro-funk-electronic-music.
2. "The Rhythm of Afrika Bambaataa," Universal Zulu Nation, accessed on April 18, 2018. new.zulunation.com/afrika-bambaataa/.
3. Quoted in Kot, "Bambaataa."
4. Quoted in Billy Jam, "Creator of the Scratch: Grand Wizard Theodore," Hip Hop Slam, 2001. www.hiphopslam.com/articles/int_grandwizardtheo.html.

Chapter Two:
Hip-Hop Goes National

5. Quoted in Jenny Eliscu, "Q&A: Mary J. Blige," *Rolling Stone*, September 4, 2003. www.rollingstone.com/music/features/mary-j-blige-20030904.
6. Jayo Felony, in-person interview with Soren Baker, April 26, 2005.
7. Quoted in Kot, "Bambaataa."
8. QD3, in-person interview with Soren Baker, March 23, 2005.
9. Quoted in Kot, "Bambaataa."
10. The Reverend Run with Curtis L. Taylor, *It's Like That: A Spiritual Memoir*. New York, NY: St. Martin's Press, 2000, p. 30.

Chapter Three:
Rap Music

11. Quoted in Austin Scaggs, "Q&A: P. Diddy," *Rolling Stone*, August 7, 2003. www.rollingstone.com/music/features/p-diddy-20030807.

HIP-HOP: A CULTURAL AND MUSICAL REVOLUTION

12. Stephen Thomas Erlewine, "Salt-N-Pepa," AllMusic, accessed on April 19, 2018. www.allmusic.com/artist/salt-n-pepa-mn0000294891/biography.
13. MC Lyte, in-person interview with Soren Baker, February 6, 2003.
14. Quoted in Reginald C. Dennis, *The Very Best of Big Daddy Kane* (liner notes). Warner Bros. Records and Rhino Entertainment, 2001.
15. Big Daddy Kane, phone interview with Soren Baker, March 2003.
16. Stephen Thomas Erlewine, "Public Enemy," AllMusic, accessed on April 19, 2018. www.allmusic.com/artist/public-enemy-mn0000856785/biography.

Chapter Four:
Introduction of Gangsta Rap

17. Schoolly D, phone interview with Soren Baker, March 2003.
18. David Mills, "Los Angeles' Gangsters of Rap, Escalating the Attitude," *Washington Post*, May 20, 1990. www.washingtonpost.com/archive/lifestyle/style/1990/05/20/los-angeles-gangsters-of-rap-escalating-the-attitude/946400da-81af-482c-9e14-a0e37f7e4be1/?utm_term=.8e0a9185814d.
19. David Mills, "Recordings," *Washington Post*, September 2, 1990. www.washingtonpost.com/archive/lifestyle/style/1990/09/02/recordings/c284a7e4-3c30-4c56-8552-44969be335c9/?utm_term=.8f83d61aeaad.
20. J. D. Considine, "Rap Capital Shifts from N.Y. to L.A.," *Baltimore Sun*, April 23, 1989, p. 1M.
21. Quoted in Newsweek Staff, "Number One with a Bullet," *Newsweek*, June 30, 1991. www.newsweek.com/number-one-bullet-204074.
22. Mills, "Los Angeles' Gangsters of Rap."
23. Richard Harrington, "Rap's Unheard Riot Warning," *Washington Post*, May 27, 1992. www.washingtonpost.com/archive/lifestyle/1992/05/27/raps-unheard-riot-warning/92410670-4406-465f-8c8d-537114d12e31/?utm_term=.36a873f781e8.
24. LL Cool J with Karen Hunter, *I Make My Own Rules*. New York, NY: St. Martin's Press, 1997, p. 196.
25. Mills, "Los Angeles' Gangsters of Rap."
26. Lorraine Ali, "The 90s Era—Smells Like Teen Spirit," *Rolling Stone*, May 15, 1997, p. 97.

27. Quoted in Laura Parker, "Rap Group Acquitted in Florida," *Washington Post*, October 21, 1990. www.washingtonpost.com/archive/politics/1990/10/21/rap-group-acquitted-in-florida/52cb05fc-03c8-4069-9c4d-d5691998a392/?utm_term=.89ae0af4428f.
28. Jonathan Yardley, "Art and the Oeuvre of 2 Live Crew," *Washington Post*, October 22, 1990, p. B2.

Chapter Five:
The Rap Business Expands
29. Julio G, phone interview with Soren Baker, March 15, 2005.
30. Phyllis Pollack, phone interview with Soren Baker, March 14, 2005.
31. Tomica Wright, phone interview with Soren Baker, March 15, 2005.
32. Layzie Bone, phone interview with Soren Baker, March 9, 2005.
33. Young Noble, phone interview with Soren Baker, March 18, 2005.

Chapter Six:
Southern Rap and the Reemergence of DJs
34. Quoted in Paul Meara, "David Banner, Freddie Gibbs Discuss Impact of OutKast's 'Southernplayalisticadillacmuzik,'" HipHopDX, April 26, 2014. hiphopdx.com/news/id.28507/title.david-banner-freddie-gibbs-discuss-impact-of-outkasts-southernplayalisticadillacmuzik.
35. Chingy, in-person interview with Soren Baker, October 27, 2004.
36. Matt Miller, "Dirty Decade: Rap Music and the US South, 1997–2007," Southernspaces.org, June 10, 2008. southernspaces.org/2008/dirty-decade-rap-music-and-us-south-1997%E2%80%932007.
37. Quoted in Hillary Crosley, "Blessed by Lil Scrappy, Produced By Lil Jon, David Banner Gets Certified," MTV.com, May 5, 2005. www.mtv.com/news/articles/1501362/david-banner-gets-certified.jhtml.
38. Lil Jon, phone interview with Soren Baker, August 2002.
39. Nicki Minaj, in-person interview with Soren Baker, March 21, 2010.
40. Quoted in Chris Mench, "The Timeline of Lil Wayne's Issues With Cash Money Records and Birdman," Complex.com, October 25, 2017. www.complex.com/music/lil-wayne-cash-money-beef-timeline/.

Chapter Seven:
The New Global Rap Landscape

41. Quoted in Dan Rys, "Hip-Hop Is Dominating Streaming—And Rappers Like Cardi B and Lil Uzi Vert Are Leading the Way," *Billboard*, September 14, 2017. www.billboard.com/articles/news/magazine-feature/7964849/cardi-b-lil-uzi-vert-hip-hop-dominating-streaming.
42. Quoted in Rys, "Hip-Hop Is Dominating Streaming."
43. Quoted in Rys, "Hip-Hop Is Dominating Streaming."
44. Quoted in Jem Aswad, "Chance the Rapper Says 'SoundCloud Is Here to Stay' In Cryptic Tweet," *Variety*, July 14, 2017. variety.com/2017/digital/news/chance-the-rapper-says-soundcloud-is-here-to-stay-in-cryptic-tweet-1202496118/.
45. Quoted in Neel V. Patel, "Why Chance the Rapper Shouted Out SoundCloud at the Grammys," Inverse, February 12, 2017. www.inverse.com/article/27749-chance-the-rapper-soundcloud-grammys.
46. Quoted in Bonsu Thompson, "How Streaming Revolutionized Rap's Album Rollouts on the Road to No. 1," NPR, September 28, 2017. www.npr.org/sections/therecord/2017/09/28/554220367/how-streaming-revolutionized-raps-album-rollouts-on-the-road-to-no-1.
47. Wiz Khalifa, phone interview with Soren Baker, February 11, 2011.
48. Quoted in Associated Press, "Tego Calderon Is the King of 'Reggaeton,'" *Today*, October 26, 2004. www.today.com/popculture/tego-calderon-king-reggaeton-wbna6339822.
49. "The Blacker the Berry," track 13 on Kendrick Lamar, *To Pimp a Butterfly*. Aftermath Entertainment, 2015.
50. Will Butler, "Six Months of Kendrick Lamar's Masterpiece, *To Pimp a Butterfly*," Gigwise, September 15, 2015. www.gigwise.com/reviews/102811/kendrick-lamar-to-pimp-a-butterfly-6-months-later-feature.
51. Quoted in Randall Colburn and Ben Kaye, "Kendrick Lamar Opens 2018 Grammys with Powerful Performance Featuring U2 and Dave Chappelle: Watch," Consequence Of Sound, January 28, 2018. consequenceofsound.net/2018/01/kendrick-lamar-opens-2018-with-powerful-medley-featuring-xxx-dna-and-new-music-watch/.

52. Quoted in Colburn and Kaye, "Kendrick Lamar Opens 2018 Grammys with Powerful Performance Featuring U2 and Dave Chappelle: Watch."
53. Matthew Trammell, "Kendrick Lamar, DAMN.," Pitchfork, April 18, 2017. pitchfork.com/reviews/albums/23147-damn/.
54. John Gotty, "Hip-Hop Is Doing Just Fine 10 Years After Nas Declared It Dead," Uproxx, December 19, 2016. uproxx.com/hiphop/nas-hip-hop-is-dead-10-year-anniversary/.
55. Quoted in Emil Wilbekin. "Art Imitates Life." *Vibe*, September 2003, p. 150.

Essential
Albums

Publisher's note: Some albums may contain strong language or explicit content.

A Tribe Called Quest
The Low End Theory (1991)

Beastie Boys
Licensed to Ill (1986)

Big Daddy Kane
Long Live the Kane (1988)

De La Soul
3 Feet High and Rising (1989)

Dr. Dre
The Chronic (1992)

Eric B. & Rakim
Paid In Full (1987)

Grandmaster Flash and the Furious Five
The Message (1982)

Ice Cube
AmeriKKKa's Most Wanted (1990)

JAY-Z
Reasonable Doubt (1996)

Kanye West
The College Dropout (2004)
Late Registration (2005)

Kendrick Lamar
DAMN. (2017)
To Pimp a Butterfly (2015)

LL Cool J
Bigger and Deffer (BAD) (1987)

Lil Jon & the East Side Boyz
Kings of Crunk (2002)

Missy "Misdemeanor" Elliott
Supa Dupa Fly (1997)

Nas
Illmatic (1994)

Nicki Minaj
Pink Friday (2010)

The Notorious B.I.G.
Ready to Die (1994)

N.W.A
Straight Outta Compton (1988)

OutKast
Southernplayalisticadillacmuzik (1994)

Public Enemy
It Takes a Nation of Millions to Hold Us Back (1988)

Queen Latifah
Black Reign (1993)

Run-DMC
Raising Hell (1986)

Salt-N-Pepa
Hot, Cool & Vicious (1986)

Schoolly D
Saturday Night!—The Album (1987)

Slick Rick
The Great Adventures of Slick Rick (1988)

Snoop Dogg
Doggystyle (1993)

2Pac
Me Against the World (1995)

TLC
CrazySexyCool (1994)
Fanmail (1999)

For More Information

Books

Bradley, Adam, and Andrew DuBois. *The Anthology of Rap*. New Haven, CT: Yale University Press, 2010.
> This book analyzes the hip-hop genre and has more than 300 rap and hip-hop lyrics from some of the genre's most important artists.

Chuck D. *Chuck D Presents This Day in Rap and Hip-hop History*. New York, NY: Hachette Book Group, 2017.
> Chuck D showcases the most influential songs and moments in hip-hop's history in this book.

JAY-Z. *Decoded*. New York: Spiegel & Grau, 2010.
> *Decoded* offers a look at the rapper's music and his life as detailed through his song lyrics and additional commentary.

Orejuela, Fernando. *Rap and Hip Hop Culture*. New York, NY: Oxford University Press, 2015.
> This book touches on the four elements of hip-hop and how they have evolved over time and influenced society.

Serrano, Shea. *The Rap Year Book: The Most Important Rap Song from Every Year Since 1979, Discussed, Debated, and Deconstructed*. New York, NY: Abrams Image, 2015.
> The most important rap songs and moments in hip-hop are analyzed in this book.

Websites

AllHipHop

www.allhiphop.com

    This website includes features, reviews, and news about what is going on in the rap world and in hip-hop culture.

Google—Interactive History of Hip-Hop

www.google.com/logos/2017/hiphop/hiphop17.html

    This Google website is an interactive DJ experience, which provides insight into the history and pioneers of hip-hop.

HipHopDX

www.hiphopdx.com

    This extensive website provides plenty of up-to-date information with rap news, music videos, album reviews, interviews, editorials, and more.

HotNewHipHop

www.hotnewhiphop.com/

    This website provides the most current hip-hop news, which is updated daily, and reviews on the newest hip-hop songs, mixtapes, and albums.

Universal Hip Hop Museum

www.uhhm.org/

    This website is dedicated to promoting the Universal Hip Hop Museum, which is devoted to preserving, showcasing, and celebrating the history of hip-hop culture from its beginnings to now.

Index

A
Above the Law, 48
Aerosmith, 32
Antoinette, 35

B
Bad Boy Entertainment, 59–61, 63–64
Bambaataa, Afrika, 14–15, 20, 25, 28, 84
Beastie Boys, 40–41, 51
beatboxing, 28
Big Daddy Kane, 36–38
Biz Markie, 44
blaxploitation, 65
Blige, Mary J., 21
Blow, Kurtis, 21, 23–24, 27, 31–32
Bone Thugs-N-Harmony, 56
Boogie Down Productions (BDP), 39–40, 44
Brand Nubian, 39
break dancing (B-boying), 6–8, 10, 14–15, 20, 25–28, 31, 73
Breakin' (movie), 27, 57
Busy Bee, 20, 24, 36

C
Cardi B, 80, 86–87
Chance the Rapper, 81
Chingy, 66
Chronic, The (Dr. Dre), 49, 59
Clinton, George, 11, 25
Common, 23
crunk, 69–71
Cypress Hill, 48

D
Daz Dillinger, 49
Death Row Records, 58–61, 63–64
De La Soul, 40
Diddy, 9, 33, 54, 59, 61–63
Disco Fever, 18
DJ D-Wrek, 75
DJ Eric B., 36
DJ Funkmaster Flex, 73–74
DJ Hollywood, 20
DJ Jazzy Jeff & the Fresh Prince, 41, 57
DJ Kay Slay, 74
DJ Kool Herc, 11–12, 15–16, 20
DJ Quik, 48
DJ Yella, 45
Doug E. Fresh, 28, 37
Drake, 72, 82
Dr. Dre, 9, 45, 48–49, 52–54, 59, 63–64, 68, 74, 82
Dungeon Family, 71

E
Eazy-E, 44–45, 48, 53–56, 59
Eminem, 68, 74

F
Fab 5 Freddy, 29, 58

Felony, Jayo, 23
50 Cent, 74–75
Foxy Brown, 68, 85
Frank 207, 11
Fresh Fest, 31
Fugees, 50

G

Gang Starr, 40
Gaye, Marvin, 11
Get Down, The (TV show), 23
Geto Boys, 44–45, 49
Ghetto Mafia, 71
graffiti, 6–8, 10–11, 15, 17, 20, 25–28, 31, 73
Grandmaster Caz, 14
Grandmaster Flash, 14, 18, 20, 22–23, 32
GrandMixer DXT, 30
Grand Wizzard Theodore, 16
Gucci Mane, 71

H

Harlem World, 18
Hill, Lauryn, 50, 86

I

Ice Cube, 45, 47–48, 55, 58, 78–79, 86
Ice-T, 44, 57–58

J

JAY-Z, 9, 54, 56, 68, 74, 82, 86
Jean Grae, 35
Joe 136, 11
Julio 204, 11
Jungle Brothers, 40

K

Kid Capri, 74–75
Kid Cudi, 69
Kid 'n Play, 57
King Tee, 41
Knight, Marion "Suge," 59, 61, 63
Kool DJ Red Alert, 27
Kool G. Rap & DJ Polo, 53
Kool Moe Dee, 24, 36
Kraftwerk, 11, 15, 25
Kurupt, 49
Kweli, Talib, 51

L

Lady of Rage, The, 35
Lamar, Kendrick, 87–88
Last Poets, 6
Lil Jon, 68, 70–71
Lil' Kim, 68, 85
Lil Uzi Vert, 71, 80
Lil Wayne, 71–72, 79, 86
Linkin Park, 75
LL Cool J, 33–35, 41, 48

M

Malone, Moses, 27
Mannie Fresh, 71
Master P, 54, 56, 68–69, 86
McDaniels, Darryl (DMC), 29
McDaniels, Ralph, 27
MC Lyte, 34–35
MC Ren, 45, 47
MCs, 17–18, 36, 38
MC Sha Rock, 35
MC Shy D, 41
Mele Mel, 20, 22–24, 30, 42
Miller, Matt, 67
Mills, David, 46–48
Missy Elliott, 86
Mizell, Jason (DJ Jam Master Jay), 29
Monie Love, 35

Moore, Rudy Ray, 6
Mos Def, 51
Ms. Melodie, 35
Mystikal, 69

N

Nas, 68, 80, 88
Native Tongues, 40
Nicki Minaj, 72, 86
Notorious B.I.G., The, 59–65
N.W.A, 44–49, 52–56, 59, 63, 68, 87

O

OutKast, 66, 71
Outlawz, 62–63

P

Poor Righteous Teachers, 39
Public Enemy, 39–40, 87

Q

Queen Latifah, 34, 40

R

Rakim, 36–37
"Rapper's Delight," (Sugarhill Gang), 7, 20–22, 24–26, 32, 73
Recording Industry Association of America (RIAA), 51
Rock Steady Crew, 15, 26–27, 75
Rock Steady Lounge, 18–19
Ross, Rick, 71, 82
Run-DMC, 28 29, 31–33, 35, 41, 55, 85
Ruthless Records, 54–56, 59

S

Salt-N-Pepa, 34–35, 41, 50
Saturday Night Live, 21–22
Schoolly D, 23, 42–43, 54
Scott-Heron, Gil, 6
Shaka Kings, 14
Shaka Queens, 14
Shanté, Roxanne, 35–37
Silkk the Shocker, 69
Simmons, Joseph (Run), 28
Slick Rick, 36–37
Smith, Will, 41, 57–58
Snoop Dogg, 48–49, 53, 58–59, 61
Soulja Boy, 77–78
SoundCloud, 80–81
Source Awards, 61
Southernplayalisticadillacmuzik (OutKast), 66
Spotify, 79–80
Stetsasonic, 40
Straight Outta Compton (album), 45, 48, 55
Straight Outta Compton (movie), 45, 63
Sugarhill Gang, 7, 20, 22–24, 32
Sugar Hill Records, 20, 22, 25, 28

T

TAKI 183, 11
T. I., 68, 71
TIDAL, 79, 82–83
T La Rock, 24
TLC, 50–51
Tribe Called Quest, A, 40
Tupac Shakur (2Pac), 8, 61–65
2 Live Crew, 44, 49–50, 52

U

Unsolved: The Murders of Tupac and The Notorious B.I.G., 63

W

Waka Flocka Flame, 71

"Walk This Way" (Aerosmith and Run-DMC), 32
WC and the Maad Circle, 48
West, Kanye, 68–69, 82–83
Wild Style (movie), 26
Wiz Khalifa, 83–84

X
X Clan, 39

Y
Yo Gotti, 71
Young Jeezy, 71

Z
Zulu Nation, 14

Picture
Credits

Cover (main) chaoss/Shutterstock.com; cover (background), back cover, pp. 3, 4, 6, 10, 20, 31, 42, 54, 65, 76, 90, 95, 97, 99, 103, 104 Zarya Maxim Alexandrovich/Shutterstock.com; p. 7 Anthony Barboza/Getty Images; p. 9 Jamie McCarthy/WireImage/Getty Images; pp. 12, 33 PYMCA/UIG via Getty Images; pp. 14, 46 Lynn Goldsmith/Corbis/VCG via Getty Images; p. 16 Johnny Nunez/WireImage/Getty Images; pp. 21, 22 Granamour Weems Collection/Alamy Stock Photo; pp. 24, 29 Bettmann/Bettmann/Getty Images; p. 26 Linda Vartoogian/Getty Images; pp. 35, 36 Michael Ochs Archives/Getty Images; p. 38 Jacques M. Chenet/Corbis/Corbis via Getty Images; p. 39 Suzie Gibbons/Redferns/Getty Images; p. 43 David Corio/Michael Ochs Archives/Getty Images; p. 51 Ron Davis/Getty Images; p. 52 Ron Galella/WireImage/Getty Images; p. 55 Al Pereira/Michael Ochs Archives/Getty Images; p. 57 GAB Archive/Redferns/Getty Images; p. 58 Gie Knaeps/Getty Images; p. 60 Chris Walter/WireImage/Getty Images; p. 62 Time Life Pictures/DMI/The LIFE Picture Collection/Getty Images; p. 66 KMazur/WireImage/Getty Images; p. 69 Kevin Winter/Getty Images; p. 70 Theo Wargo/WireImage/Getty Images; p. 72 Prince Williams/WireImage/Getty Images; p. 75 Robert Lachman/Los Angeles Times via Getty Images; p. 77 Noel Vasquez/Getty Images; p. 81 MARK RALSTON/AFP/Getty Images; p. 84 Joe Seer/Shutterstock.com; p. 87 MTV/TRL/Getty Images; p. 88 Scott Dudelson/Getty Images for Coachella.

About the Author

Vanessa Oswald is an experienced freelance writer and editor who has written pieces for publications based in New York City and the Western New York area, which include *Resource* magazine, *The Public*, *Auxiliary* magazine, and *Niagara Gazette*. In her spare time she enjoys dancing, traveling, reading, snowboarding, and attending live concerts.